management
institute
inspiring leaders

COACHING

MATT SOMERS

The publisher has used its best endeavours to ensure that the URLs for external websites referred to in this book are correct and active at the time of going to press. However, the publisher and the author have no responsibility for the websites and can make no guarantee that a site will remain live or that the content will remain relevant, decent or appropriate.

Orders: Please contact Bookpoint Ltd, 130 Milton Park, Abingdon, Oxon OX14 4SB. Telephone: (44) 01235 827720, Fax: (44) 01235 400454. Lines are open from 9.00 to 5.00, Monday to Saturday, with a 24-hour message answering service. You can also order through our website www.hoddereducation.co.uk.

British Library Cataloguing in Publication Data
A catalogue record for this title is available from the British Library.

ISBN-13: 978 0340 959 039

First published 2008
Impression number 10 9 8 7 6 5 4 3 2 1
Year 2012 2011 2010 2009 2008

Typeset by Transet Limited, Coventry, England.
Printed in Great Britain for Hodder Education, part of Hachette Livre UK, 338 Euston Road, London NW1 3BH by Cox & Wyman Ltd, Reading, Berkshire.

Hachette Livre UK's policy is to use papers that are natural, renewable and recyclable products and made from wood grown in sustainable forests. The logging and manufacturing processes are expected to conform to the environmental regulations of the country of origin.

chartered
management
institute
inspiring leaders

Chartered Manager

Transform the way you work

The Chartered Management Institute's Chartered Manager award is the ultimate accolade for practising professional managers. Designed to transform the way you think about your work and how you add value to your organisation, it is based on demonstrating measurable impact.

This unique award proves your ability to make a real difference in the workplace.

Chartered Manager focuses on the six vital business skills of:

- Leading people
- Managing change
- Meeting customer needs
- Managing information and knowledge
- Managing activities and resources
- Managing yourself

Transform your organisation

There is a clear and well-established link between good management and improved organisational performance. Recognising this, the Chartered Manager scheme requires individuals to demonstrate how they are applying their leadership and change management skills to make significant impact within their organisation.

Transform your career

Whatever career stage a manager is at Chartered Manager will set them apart. Chartered Manager has proven to be a stimulus to career progression, either via recognition by their current employer or through the motivation to move on to more challenging roles with new employers.

But don't take just our word for it …

Chartered Manager has transformed the careers and organisations of managers in all sectors.

- *'Being a Chartered Manager was one of the main contributing factors which led to my recent promotion.'*

  Lloyd Ross, Programme Delivery Manager, British Nuclear Fuels

- *'I am quite sure that a part of the reason for my success in achieving my appointment was due to my Chartered Manager award which provided excellent, independent evidence that I was a high quality manager.'*

  Donaree Marshall, Head of Programme Management Office, Water Service, Belfast

- *'The whole process has been very positive, giving me confidence in my strengths as a manager but also helping me to identify the areas of my skills that I want to develop. I am delighted and proud to have the accolade of Chartered Manager.'*

  Allen Hudson, School Support Services Manager, Dudley Metropolitan County Council

- *'As we are in a time of profound change, I believe that I have, as a result of my change management skills, been able to provide leadership to my staff. Indeed, I took over three teams and carefully built an integrated team, which is beginning to perform really well. I believe that the process I went through to gain Chartered Manager status assisted me in achieving this and consequently was of considerable benefit to my organisation.'*

  George Smart, SPO and D/Head of Resettlement, HM Prison Swaleside

To find out more or to request further information please visit our website **www.managers.org.uk/cmgr** or call us on **01536 207429**.

Contents

CHAPTER 05

CHAPTER 06

CHAPTER 07

CHAPTER 08

Preface

A tale of two managers

A long time ago in an organisation far, far, away...

Let me introduce Sam and Gene. They are both managers in a Business Development Agency. They each run teams of advisers whose job it is to interact with the business community offering advice and guidance and, where appropriate, grant funding for business development projects.

Actually none of that is true; I made it up. Sam and Gene are fictional, but their characteristics are an amalgam of many managers I have known. I think you'll recognise them too. They could work in any organisation: large or small; private or public; profit-making or not. Their problems are with the people side of their work and this is what we shall concern ourselves with as well. Sam and Gene are male but that too is irrelevant to the tale and certainly does not explain the mixed fortunes they enjoy. We'll also say that they are of a similar age, background and level of educational achievement.

Let's start with Gene. It is Gene's opinion that success is a result of a strong management style. He likes to give clear, precise instructions to his team so that nobody is uncertain about what is required. A highly competitive man in all aspects, Gene likes to win and encourages his team to be similarly motivated. He has a low tolerance for mistakes so his team tends to check and re-check all work. This takes time and makes output poor, but accuracy is good and the tellings off are few. In the short term Gene gets results, but throughout his career he has been frustrated by the tendency for results to tail off and worsen over time. He feels his teams become complacent and lazy too quickly and that he has to drive them harder and harder just to maintain standards.

Sam is also convinced that success is a result of a strong management style. He likes to engage with the members of his team as much as he can and finds that when he asks questions and gets his people thinking, they seem to take more ownership for problems and approach their work with more enthusiasm and innovation. When errors occur, Sam likes to make sure that lessons are learned and the same mistakes never occur twice in his team. Sam's reputation is as a long-game player. His senior managers know they have to be patient but Sam gets spectacular results in the end. For his part, Sam is frustrated that results are so long in coming and wishes there was a way to speed things up.

There was no talk of coaching in Sam and Gene's day, but it was undoubtedly a feature of Sam's style and a missing component of Gene's. Whilst they each enjoyed success it was Sam who prevailed over the long term. With an even better understanding of coaching, Sam could have accelerated his results and Gene – if he added coaching to his skill set – could have used his obvious strengths to even greater effect, and over the longer term.

This is a little book about coaching. It does not pretend to offer you a silver bullet to slay all your people problems and it does not suggest that coaching is a panacea to solve all workplace ills. It does offer straightforward, practical, proven tactics for using coaching to get results through people, which in the end is the essence of management in my view.

So whether you're a Gene or a Sam or somewhere on the spectrum between the two, I hope you will find ideas here to become a manager who coaches and thus a manager who is successful.

How to use this book

You'll have seen from the contents page that the book is divided into ten chapters. If you're new to coaching, I would recommend that you read the book cover to cover. If you've had some coaching experience or read up on it before, you may prefer to read single chapters. With this in mind I have tried to make each chapter 'stand alone' and I hope you will forgive the repetition that this requires.

Whatever your preference, please remember that you cannot acquire coaching skills without practice. It is vital that you try out the techniques and ideas described so that you can absorb them in your own way. You will undoubtedly make mistakes along the way, but this is how you'll learn. The people whom you coach will come to no harm provided you're honest in what you're doing and that you genuinely set out to help them move forward.

01

What is coaching?

Introduction

Everybody's talking about coaching these days, but what does it mean? Isn't it what football managers do? Well it might be, but these days football managers seem to have an army of separate defence coaches, goalkeeping coaches and so on, so that's not a helpful comparison. Perhaps you've seen a life coach on daytime TV or read a life coaching, self-help type book. There might be a useful definition to be extrapolated from life coaching, but in a business context we've rarely the time or the expertise to delve into personal, lifestyle issues. Becoming a manager who coaches must require us to use coaching in a very different context.

This chapter is about setting a foundation for all the information that follows. Before we can begin to develop our coaching skills we must have a clear understanding of precisely what coaching is, but this is not as easy as it may seem. Coaching is an emerging area of Human Resource Development (HRD). It draws upon a very wide range of influences, from sport to psychotherapy, and it is changing every day. We must arrive at a working definition which helps you to recognise exactly what coaching is and what it isn't and how you can weave coaching into your existing set of management skills.

I will not be inviting you to discard what you already know about managing people, but I do hope to offer concepts and techniques that give you fresh options and new ideas when things seem difficult or the going gets tough. Equally I hope to show you the way to take your team's development to new heights, in the words of one of my course participants:

> *I've turned to coaching because I've taught them all I know, but I know they're still capable of more.*

Coaching defined

My *Collins English Dictionary* defines the verb to coach as 'to instruct by private tutoring, to instruct and train, to act as a coach'. This is too loose a definition to be useful, and is contaminated by references to training and instructing which might prove confusing as we'll see later on.

Let's instead turn to a couple of well-known writers in the coaching field for their views:

> *Unlocking a person's potential to maximise their performance.*
>
> John Whitmore, *Coaching for Performance*
> (Nicholas Brealey, 2002)

From this definition we can see that coaching is an activity designed to help improve someone else's performance. A comparison can be drawn with the world of sport, where coaches try to get the best out of their team without actually being on the field of play. In modern organisations, coaching must also involve turning work situations into learning opportunities as this is increasingly seen as an important part of what it is to manage.

> *Developing a person's skills and knowledge so that their job performance improves, hopefully leading to achievement of organisational objectives. It targets high performance and improvement at work, although it may have an impact on an individual's private life. It usually lasts for a short period and focuses on specific skills and goals.*
>
> Jessica Jarvis, *The Case for Coaching* (CIPD, 2006)

Some definitions suggest that coaching is purely the support and guidance provided for individuals to enable them to apply their existing skills more effectively and thus improve their job performance at work, but most include the learning theme by suggesting that coaching aims to enhance the performance and learning ability of people at the same time. A good number of definitions cite techniques such as motivation, effective questioning and deliberately matching our management style to the coachee's (person being coached) readiness to perform a particular task. We can conclude that coaching is based on helping coachees to help themselves, but that it does not rely on a one-way flow of telling and instructing.

It seems that coaching is a means of systematically increasing the capability and performance of people at work by exposing them to work-based tasks or experiences that will provide relevant learning opportunities, and making sure that learning is accessible to them later on. It is about performing *and* learning.

As far as the learning part is concerned, coaching is very different from teaching or instructing. The coach encourages people to learn for themselves; the coach usually takes a 'back seat' role, while still being able to give guidance and help when people really need it. Coaches help their teams to review experiences regularly so that they understand what has been learned.

There appears to be no universally accepted definition of the term coaching and, as described below, when it is placed alongside other development interventions an exact definition becomes even more difficult.

However, a synthesis of the numerous definitions out there identifies three elements that can constitute a working definition for this book:

- Coach and coachee establish a relationship based on trust that has the intention of improving the coachee's performance at work.
- Coaching thus becomes a process that is centred on the coachee but focused on performance.
- Coaching is a learnt skill and an essential element of the managerial role in these changing times.

Let's develop these ideas a stage further now by considering the similarities and differences between coaching and other ways of dealing with matters of performance and learning at work.

Coaching v. managing

It is again difficult to decide on a single definition of the word 'management' and this is not helped by the modern trend in organisations to label almost everything and everybody as management in some way. Arguably, everybody in an organisation *is* a manager to the extent that management is about deploying resources to get the job done. However, most would agree that a manager in an organisation has some degree of responsibility for people and some say in how those people go about their work.

With this in mind, it follows that managers *are* coaches and always have been; it's just that not all managers realise this and many would prefer it were not the case. However, if you are a manager with responsibility for people, then you need to understand what good coaching is all about and should be congratulated for investing in this book!

The most prevalent management style – even now – is a command and control type approach. Management structures for most of the last century were modelled on the military and, despite the advent of 'flat structures', 'matrix management' and the like, this is still the most common approach and feeds the appetite for command and control. Command and control – or telling people what to do and how to do it – works well in dangerous situations, emergencies or where there is no time for anything else. However, it does little for learning and enjoyment at work and thus becomes hard to sustain and causes resentment and poor performance in the end. Why does it persist? Because so many of our role models behave like this, reward structures are geared towards short-term results and because, until recently, there was a lack of a viable alternative.

Coaching has changed all this and gives us great cause for optimism. Coaching is still about mobilising people to get things done, but in a way that recognises that people are complex, living, feeling human beings and that these factors cannot be ignored.

Managers are coaches and coaches are managers. It is perfectly possible to combine both roles though not always wise to do so. There is an imbalance of power, with managers having more power and resources than the people in their teams. This is not an insurmountable barrier to coaching but it cannot be ignored.

Coaching v. instructing

Within the manager's role lie the tasks of enabling the people whom they manage to do the job and further developing those talents so that they do the job well. This is most commonly achieved by a teaching, instructing type approach. By this I mean the manager will sit with their member of staff explaining what they need to do and how they need to do it. Perhaps this is so common because we are programmed from school to believe that telling and instructing are the most appropriate way of passing on skills. There is a time and a place for instructing of course, but in the modern world of work this orthodox approach has three flaws.

Firstly, it requires that you, as a manager know how you get results yourself. You probably do for the technical aspects of your role, but what about subtle behavioural aspects of performance? If you're naturally assertive, intuitive, likeable, confident, bold or whatever it can be virtually impossible to identify how it is exactly that you're good at those things and frustrating to try and help others become adept at things you find easy. Some of the best football players become the worst managers.

The second problem to overcome is then finding words to pass that knowledge on. Let's say you can identify how exactly you behave in an assertive way or go about accessing your intuition, how do you communicate that in words? Imagine trying to explain snow to an Arab or sand to an Eskimo. The problem is that other people seldom share our frame of reference, sometimes referred to as our 'model of the world'. We have to explain things in a way that fits with other people's experience, but do so by drawing on our own unique experience. The chances of getting this right are slim, and the likelihood is that something will get lost in translation.

The third challenge is recall. There is a host of research that shows it's very difficult for people to remember what they have only ever been told or shown. One study suggests that people have forgotten almost all of anything only ever explained to them after about three months. This improves if we tell *and* show, but in order to demonstrate to our staff what we need them to do, we have to be able to do it ourselves. With the pace of change these days that's virtually impossible and is not the wisest use of our management time anyway.

Even if you are able to overcome these obstacles, an instructing type approach may still not be appropriate. It is vital to find ways of developing the people you manage using methods that are suited to their own particular skills and talents.

Since the early 1990s managers have increasingly acknowledged the need for a coaching approach in the workplace. However, there is still more telling and instructing than we need and it is important to explore the shortcomings of this approach.

Coaching v. training

- *'You've done a bit of that coaching stuff, see if you can pull a bit of a training workshop together for the team.'*
- *'There's not much classroom training going on in the summer, so put yourself about and do some one-to-one coaching instead.'*
- *'I like that coach we hired, see if we can get her to deliver the customer service workshops.'*

Whilst I won't pretend that they are direct quotes, these senior management style comments do serve to illustrate the foggy understanding of the differences between training and coaching and suggest some of the difficulties that might be encountered in moving from one discipline to the other.

Coaching is not one-to-one training ('Sitting by Nellie') and training is not group coaching. While both are ultimately concerned with making people bigger and better at what they do, training is a teacher-centred approach best deployed when a performance gap to do with a lack of knowledge or skill has been identified. Coaching on the other hand is a learner-centred approach that is best used in addressing performance gaps that are to do with attitude or state of mind.

Classroom trainers have always been asked to carry out one-to-one training when the need arises and that practice still happens. The problem is calling this activity 'coaching'. I remember being invited to watch some coaching take place in a call centre. This consisted of a sales trainer listening in on an adviser's call and afterwards pointing out the mistakes that had been made and the sales leads that had been missed. This is not coaching. At best it is feedback, at worst it is destructive criticism.

What if we want our trainers to be coaches too? Trainers know about learning styles, differing speeds of learning, engaging the learner by asking questions and so on. The good news is that as coaches they will definitely need to be drawing on their skills in these areas.

The bad news is that a lot of other things they do as a trainer will be counterproductive as a coach. The most obvious of these being telling and instructing. In training – particularly technical training – these are vital skills and we use them to pass on information and check that we have been understood. In coaching we're more concerned with helping learners find their own way forward and are probably best advised to avoid telling and instructing as far as possible. This is because when we tell or instruct we assume responsibility for making the learning happen, we deny our learners the opportunity to think for themselves and, as we saw with instructing, we end up simply passing on our recipe which is unlikely to be quite as appropriate for our learner anyway.

A desire to help people achieve their own results is a useful starting point, but the best advice for the trainer cum budding coach is to undertake some coach training.

Coaching v. mentoring

More fuss has been made about the distinction between coaching and mentoring than most other facets of coaching put together. I don't want to add to this fuss and would stress again: to the coachee or the mentee the difference is meaningless as long as they are getting the help they need. However, since this chapter is about clarifying definitions, I will attempt to draw out the differences between the two so that you are clear and so you have an intelligent answer should anyone ever ask you the question.

Like teaching or instructing, mentoring is essentially development through exchange of wisdom, with the wisdom moving from the more experienced, usually older, manager to the less experienced, usually younger, protégé. To be a mentor therefore requires us to have 'been there, worn the t-shirt', so to speak. Mentoring is very popular amongst businesses that seek quickly to guide talented employees into the top jobs. It often goes hand in hand with highly structured graduate development schemes.

Mentoring is seldom concerned with day-to-day operational issues, as these are the responsibility of the line manager. Mentoring is normally more focused on long-term development matters and, as such, mentors are often selected from outside the direct reporting line of the mentee. This has a particular advantage of course, if it is relationships within the reporting line that are proving problematic for the mentee.

Coaching – as we'll see in detail later – does not rely on the coach being more experienced than the coachee. In fact, coaching does not require any background knowledge of the issue at hand at all. Indeed some of the best coaching I've witnessed happens when the coach knows nothing at all of the situation their coachee describes and thus their coaching is more pure, uncontaminated by their own experiences.

Coaches too are often selected from outside the reporting line although I personally believe it is often easier to combine the roles of manager and coach than it is of coach and mentor.

In the end, perhaps it is more useful to consider the similarities than the differences. Coaches and mentors are both concerned with the growth of other people. Their rewards come from seeing the people they work with grow and develop; they are not driven by ego. Coaches and mentors both set store by their ability to listen and to ask questions designed to help people think. The skills and attributes of coaches and mentors are very similar. A mentoring session may provide opportunities to coach and a coaching session a chance for mentoring. Good coaches usually make good mentors and vice versa.

The European Mentoring and Coaching Council (EMCC) has given up trying to separate the two, hence the name. The Coaching and Mentoring Network similarly combines the two and organisations may be best advised to adopt a similar tactic (website details can be found on page 186).

Coaching v. counselling

I've heard it said that, apart from the spelling, there is no difference between coaching and counselling. There's a degree of truth in this but, again for the sake of clarity, I'm going to point out the differences such as they are. In fairness, it's relatively easy for me to do this as I am concentrating on coaching that takes place at work, usually delivered by the line manager. We'll see later on when we come to look at the different types and branches of coaching activity that the lines of distinction do become far more blurred.

As with mentoring, the skills of the coach and the counsellor are the same. They each listen, ask questions and offer observations in the spirit of helping their 'clients' find their own solutions. Neither coach nor counsellor would go down the 'You should...', 'You must...' route. The difference does not lie in the skill set; it is more to do with the content of the conversation and the desired outcome.

Counsellors are concerned with identifying root causes. They will guide us on a journey through our past to identify problems and critical incidents that have left a mark and cause us problems still. With such issues identified, the work of the counsellor develops into one of exploring ways of dealing with those problems and making changes. We can easily see that relationship counsellors, substance abuse counsellors, bereavement counsellors, etc. focus on *dealing with what's happened*.

Coaches are concerned with moving forward. Coaches help their coachees to identify a desired set of circumstances, to examine how that contrasts with current circumstances and then to plan out a series of steps to get from one point to the other. The coach starts from the here and now and, although aware that situations in the past can cause problems today, is more focused on creating mobility and momentum and on getting people started. Coaches focus on *dealing with what must happen next.*

Imagine you're playing in a football match and your team is 3–0 down at half time. The team counsellor would examine the mistakes of the first half, but the team coach will set out the tactics for the second. Both are useful, and as ever are often combined. As always, the needs of the people we help trump any academic debate around the differences.

However, getting the positioning right is crucial. I've seen many a coaching programme get off to a shaky start because staff perceived that they were going to be counselled and were obviously uneasy about how well their managers were qualified to offer this kind of help and whether it was appropriate to talk about potentially emotive personal issues in a work context. There may be a time for counselling at work of course, and what starts out as a coaching session may move in that direction. With this in mind it is worth checking out your organisation's welfare and access to counselling policy if you have the slightest suspicion that a coaching approach may uncover a deep-seated issue and thus need a professional intervention.

Coaching compared

The following compares all these forms of workplace development in their simplest terms:

Managing	'Do this.'
Instructing	'Here's how to do this.'
Training	'Have a go at doing this.'
Mentoring	'My advice would be to...'
Counselling	'What feelings does this invoke?'
Coaching	'How do you think you could...?'

An appreciation of these similarities and differences is useful when it comes to positioning coaching in your team and in your organisation. You may well find that if your team is unclear about what coaching involves, then they may not engage as fully as you'd wish.

Comparing coaching to these others forms of workplace development and people development methods has helped us understand coaching *relative* to other approaches, but let's now refine our understanding of coaching in absolute terms.

Coaching is...

Coaching is about helping people move out of their comfort zones (see Figure 1.1).

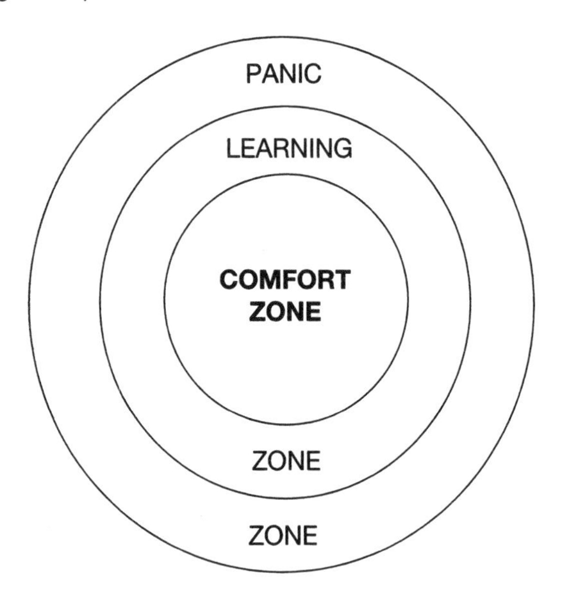

Figure 1.1: Moving from the comfort zone to the learning zone

By definition, we are working in our comfort zone when we are performing tasks and activities we find relatively easy and straightforward. Many would argue that there is absolutely nothing wrong with people operating in their comfort zone provided the job gets done, and that not everybody is hell bent on climbing the greasy pole chasing promotion after promotion. This is true, but it is less true than it once was. In these changing times the work that people are comfortable with will change even if they don't and thus we have to help our teams to constantly renew their knowledge and skills. All too often we handle this badly and move people too quickly from comfort zone to panic zone without recognising the learning zone in-between.

Coaching is about releasing potential. As coaches we make the assumption that people come equipped and hard-wired with all they need to succeed. The coaching principles and techniques we'll explore in depth later on are about removing the barriers to that potential coming through. Thus coaching can be thought of as more concerned with *drawing out* than *putting in*.

Most conventional training and development concentrates on teaching people the skills and knowledge they need to perform. Coaching follows on from this and concentrates on giving people the means to develop their knowledge and skills; to have access to them even when under pressure and to apply them in a diverse range of situations. Coaching then is more focused on *helping others to learn* as this is a much more enduring outcome and one which creates independence.

Done well, coaching should be motivational and enjoyable for coach and coachee alike. The coach will get their kicks from observing their people blossom and noticing the delight people feel as they grow, develop, solve and innovate within a coaching relationship. In a work situation, coaching has to be *performance focused*. There are targets to be reached, sales to be made, costs to be contained, clients to serve, changes to be made, policies to implement and so on. It is only because coaching has proven such an effective contributor to these ends that it has endured and not fallen away in the manner of so many fads. But coaching is also *people centred*. In the end, it is people who perform (or don't) and we must remember that people come with feelings, emotions, hopes and fears, etc. and that any approach to dealing with people that ignores this fact is doomed to fail.

Coaching is not...

Coaching should never be simply telling people what to do and how to do it – this is teaching or instructing. That's not to say that there's never a place for 'telling' in a work situation, it's just that we shouldn't call it coaching. It may well be that if someone is new to the team or just generally inexperienced then our management style needs to involve more telling at the start. However, once the people that we work with have a decent level of knowledge and skill, telling becomes counterproductive because those same people will instinctively want to use their knowledge and skills as best they can and seek to exercise a little initiative and independence. If we carry on telling, we stifle those instincts and end up with a frustrated team of 'yes men'. We can use coaching to help people develop their knowledge and skills in their own unique way and encourage them to develop further still.

Coaching is not about offering uninvited feedback. Many of the organisations I work with claim to have an established coaching set-up, but are mystified by its patchy results. Closer examination reveals that what goes on in the name of coaching is anything but. Staff are observed in action and then a manager or a so-called 'coach' – usually clutching a clipboard – takes them off to a private room and runs through a list of mistakes made or opportunities missed. This kind of clumsy feedback does more harm than good and at worst can stoke up resentment and a desire to seek revenge or 'get management back'. A coach, on the other hand offers feedback free from judgement and places much more importance on what the staff member had noticed during the interaction in question.

As a coach you are not obliged to rescue people and have all the answers. This is an easy trap to fall into for the inexperienced coach and creates a lot of pressure. It may well be that despite a lengthy coaching conversation or a series of them, a problem remains unsolved or a coachee is no further forward. This does not mean that the coaching has failed or that the coach has done anything wrong. I stress again: coaching is not a magic panacea to cure all workplace ills. Some work problems are complex, multi-part and not easily solved. Some people that you coach may have given up in spirit if not in body and put themselves beyond the reach of even the greatest coach. You can rest assured that a bit of decent coaching can't do any harm and will usually do at least some good.

Coaching is most certainly not only for poor performers, and to position it as such is a mistake. A sure way to kill off coaching in its infancy in an organisation is to introduce it alongside a performance management system or disciplinary process. Alternatively, to introduce coaching by encouraging the already top performers to develop even further, sends much more positive signals and positions coaching as about moving forward; irrespective of your starting point.

Different types of coaching

Coaching draws on many different influences. For most people the word itself is connected with sporting activities and it is easy to understand how the relationship between performer and coach works in that setting. The sporting connection also offers some useful comparisons that can help make the case for coaching. Sports coaches are rarely better performers than the people whom they coach. In fact, many top sports coaches these days were fairly average performers in their field, but recognise that good coaching is not about passing on skills but about being a catalyst for the development of the coachee(s). Coaching also draws on many principles from psychotherapy, such as the need to establish the boundaries of the working relationship and the importance of active listening. In coaching at work we can also see many parallels with organisation development and management training. Many of the structured psychological models such as Neuro-Linguistic Programming (NLP) and Transactional Analysis (TA), have also enjoyed something of a renaissance alongside the rising popularity of coaching.

I believe that it is these diverse influences that have led to the fragmentation of the coaching approach and the different branches of the profession that are emerging. For the purposes of this section I will concentrate on the main three:

- **Life coaching.** This normally takes place at the behest of an individual who wants some help in resolving issues in one or more parts of their personal life. This can often involve coaching around relationship difficulties, making a career change, retirement or any of life's significant turning points. Where the Life Coach uncovers some deep-rooted, serious issue, such as physical abuse or spiralling debt, they will normally refer their client for more specialist help.
- **Executive coaching.**Which is normally brought in to help the senior team manage a piece of significant change such as a merger or acquisition. Many Executive Coaches are accomplished business people themselves and probably need that credibility to get through the door and make a start. It follows that much of what they do can be thought of as more like consultancy than the coaching I've described here, but that is of little consequence to the executive who feels they've been helped.
- **Manager-coaching.** This is coaching undertaken by the manager or team leader as part and parcel of their role and for the benefit of their team members. This is the most impactful type of coaching in my view and the one on which the rest of this book will concentrate.

Despite the variety of influences and the differing types of coaching now on offer, there appears to be a number of common elements that create a philosophy of coaching. Coaching reflects the *humanistic* branch of psychology in that its intention is to bring about the release of potential. There is a nod toward *existentialism* in the notion that people are not hapless victims but always have choice and that their behaviour is a result of the choices they make. We can see a lot of *Eastern influences* in coaching in the emphasis placed on operating in the present, and in the belief that people are equipped with all that they need to be productive. Finally, coaching adheres to the *constructivist* principle that there is no one single version of truth or reality.

Summary

This chapter has been about putting boundaries around coaching so that we can understand how it fits with the other things we do as part of people management. The purpose of managing people at work is to get the job done well and help our team members take advantage of any opportunities that doing the job well presents. Coaching encompasses both of these points because it is performance focused but person centred.

We've seen that coaching shares aspects of instructing, mentoring, counselling and so on but also has important distinctions. Coaching requires no expertise or background on the part of the coach. Whilst instructing and training are effective at developing initial skills and abilities, coaching has proven the most effective way of developing higher skills once people have reached a point where they need to develop in their own unique way. In truth, a good coach – in the widest sense of the term – will probably move from 'tell' to 'coach' and back again within the course of any coaching relationship. Their concern will be with developing people, not with labelling the type of development they're doing.

Coaching draws on a wide range of influences such as sport, management development and the helping professions. This has led to a fragmenting of the profession and the emergence of specialisms such as life coaching and executive coaching. However, all coaching has unifying principles, including recognising different versions of reality, working in the present and seeing the individual as resourceful, with all the potential they need to achieve their goals.

INSTANT TIP

Before you do anything else, get together with the people whom you'll coach and decide on a working definition for yourselves. It doesn't matter if your version doesn't quite match an official definition but it must provide a consistent approach that everyone can follow.

02

Why do we need coaching?

Introduction

There are several obvious reasons why an organisation may be keen to include coaching in a suite of Human Resource Development interventions. It usually takes place in the actual work setting and so, not only does this avoid the expense in terms of time and money of the traditional classroom event, it means that coaching is rooted in a genuine 'live' situation. As described earlier, coaching is a learnt skill and so regular coaching sessions will also be developmental for the coach as well as the coachee.

Before we get into the detail of these and other reasons for coaching, let's once again consider some more authoritative views. John Whitmore, the UK's leading voice on coaching, lists the benefits of coaching as follows:

- *Improved performance and productivity – given that coaching brings out the best in individuals and teams.*

- *Improved relationships – since the questioning style he advocates clearly values the coachee and his/her answer.*
- *More time for the manager – based on the argument that those who are coached welcome responsibility and do not have to be chased or watched.*
- *Greater flexibility and adaptability to change – given that coaching is about being responsive as well as responsible.*

John Whitmore, *Coaching for Performance* (Nicholas Brealey, 2002)

Many advance this argument by suggesting that coaching produces results which are not only desirable, but an absolute necessity in today's environment. Peter M. Pay, the former European Training Manager for ICI and now an independent consultant described its relevance as follows:

> *In a modern, high performance world, every organisation requires highly competent staff, who frequently provide its principal 'competitive edge'. Without skilled, motivated and confident employees, few organisations will succeed in the long term. Training alone cannot hope to deliver this fully, especially since it is generally accepted that as much as 80 per cent of work related training is actually acquired on the job. Staff need to be encouraged, enabled, supported and guided to obtain such learning while working. This is what coaching should provide.*

Peter M. Pay, *The Coaching Challenge* (*Organisations and People*, 1995)

It is worth noting that Pay goes on to point out that 'off the job' training should not be abandoned but supported by good coaching so that development needs, large and small, can be facilitated and met.

A further point is added to the benefits described above by Bernard Redshaw, an independent management training consultant, who claims that when good coaching is widespread, the whole organisation can learn new things more quickly, and can therefore adapt to change more effectively. Furthermore, coaching tends to be self-perpetuating in that people who are well coached readily become good coaches themselves. So the more coaches an organisation has, the more it keeps on producing them.

The rest of this chapter then is concerned with putting forward a detailed and hopefully convincing argument for coaching in organisations. I hope these points will help you convince both the sceptical coachee and the circumspect senior team – who will need to be convinced that coaching creates value if they are to release the resources needed.

Making the case for coaching

Let's now explore in detail the factors that I believe make the case for coaching a compelling one.

These days employees expect to be developed. HR people mumble (and sometimes grumble) about something called the psychological contract. This is an unwritten, tacit contract that sits alongside the formal, written employment contract and is just as important. The employment contract sets out the basic consideration, which will be along the lines of 'if you do what we ask, we'll pay you £X'. In reality things are of course more complex and the nature of the work required will be detailed in job descriptions and the like, while the reward part will be similarly defined as salary, bonus, etc. and a range of non-financial rewards such as holidays. The psychological contract is each party's understanding of what each other will do to play 'fair'. For most of the twentieth century this contract ran along the lines of 'turn up for work and do a reasonable job and we'll employ you for life.' However, working life has been undergoing some sort of transformation since the 1980s, and the 'job for life' no longer exists. Today it is probably impossible and certainly unwise to assume that we will have only one or two employers throughout our working life. The psychological contract these days runs along the lines of 'in exchange for my efforts at work I expect to be developed and build my CV so that I increase my overall employment prospects'. In the UK at the time of writing, there is also virtually full employment and a scarcity of skills which means that employers are having to work harder to recruit and retain the best people – the so-called war for talent. This makes the job market a seller's market with potential employees in a strong bargaining position. Recruitment firms even talk of the 'reverse interview' where candidates size up their chances of development before considering whether to accept any offer. To match this expectation with only orthodox training and development (e.g. classroom training and external qualifications) would be dreadfully expensive and ultimately unworkable. There will always be a place for such things in an overall learning and development strategy of course, but coaching – particularly when delivered by managers – provides a more timely, cost-effective and tailor-made solution.

The change to the psychological contract is but one of myriad changes that have been played out in the theatre of work in the last few years. The current industrial relations climate sees the pendulum swinging back towards the employee and their rights, with some employers bemoaning the bureaucracy and red-tape that this entails. Nonetheless it seems that family-friendly policies such as parental leave and fexible working are here to stay, driven at least in part by people's desire to want a better work–life balance.

Other social changes have had an impact on working life too. Work now occupies a very different place in people's lives. Where once work was simply the way we made enough money to pay the bills, we now work for a host of psychological as well as economic reasons. For example many people now fulfil their need for social interaction through work – probably because of the amount of time we spend there! Others fulfil their esteem needs through work, enjoying the satisfaction that comes from doing meaningful work and doing it well. It's as if collectively we've all moved up a level or two on Maslow's hierarchy of needs (see Chapter 3). In Western economies in general and in the UK in particular it is unlikely that anyone is going to fall on really hard times if they're out of work – we have a welfare system that provides support, so a management style that invites people to be thankful they receive a salary is unlikely to prove very motivating. Instead we need to recognise that we need a more human approach that captures the variety of reasons why people come to work. Corporate Social Responsibility (CSR) is a start but there is much work to do at the level of the fundamental relationship between the manager and their team.

There is now much more job mobility than was once the case and I don't just mean moving from one company to another. Where once the staff of offices, factories and shops could all be found in a single building, it is now typical to find workforces dispersed across several locations. This may mean you managing teams with members in different parts of the country or even different parts of the world. You may have people in your team who have an almost entirely different work pattern to your own and whom you hardly ever see. You may have to manage people who work from home at the same time as people who sit at the desk opposite yours. In the face of this we need a flexible management style that relies on empowering people to use their initiative and make things happen rather than waiting for you, the manager, to call all the shots. In short, we need a coaching approach.

At the broadest level there are the massive changes being caused by globalisation and worldwide competition. We are doomed if we continue to rely on business models based purely on financial considerations. The deployment of an organisation's people is increasingly being seen as a vital part of its chances of success, and there are moves for learning and development to be reported on in the annual report alongside profit and loss. Finally, there are the changes we have witnessed – and will continue to have to manage – from the relentless march of technology.

The Internet and World Wide Web present a host of opportunities to be successful and improve the way we work, but only if we're prepared to recognise that we, as managers, cannot keep pace with our staff who are actually using the new technologies day-in and day-out. As the great business strategist Gary Hammel once said, 'In the knowledge economy those who live by the sword will be shot by those who don't.'

Against the background of these changes, organisations have had to change their structures, processes and procedures. The days of fixed reporting lines seem gone forever; it is much more typical now to find people reporting to several managers. A lot of clerical work, to take one example, is now project based, meaning over a period of time the same employee could be working for and accountable to several different managers. Similarly, somebody working in say IT may be involved in installation projects for a number of different departments and answerable to several different managers at once, each with their own requirements and management style and each convinced of course that theirs is the most important project and deserving of the highest priority. There are also people whose relationship with the organisation as a whole is looser and far less formal than used to be the case. Go to any modern contact centre for example and you'll find full-time staff, part-time staff and agency staff rubbing shoulders and handling customer calls. You'll find interim managers and consultants occupying management roles, and freelance professionals peppered around the training, marketing and IT departments. This all makes the modern workplace a far more dynamic and interesting place to operate, but requires new ways of working.

Much has been written on the effect of these changes on the modern employee. We know that stress is on the rise, sickness absence at an all-time high and the changing of jobs in search of something better much more common. But what of you the poor old manager? How can you cultivate the motivation and efforts of a group of people whom you really rely on but over whom you have no formal authority at all? How can you help a team focus on the key outcomes of your project when after each meeting they each return to their line managers who put them under pressure to concentrate on the 'day job'? You can't operate any kind of 'command and control' type approach when you have no mandate to do so and when you can be constantly undermined by those that do. You need instead to utilise your moral authority, to engage with your people as equals and to operate as a manager who is able to get people focused, help them to manage possibly conflicting priorities and provide the learning opportunities that are becoming so highly prized. You need, in other words, to become a coach.

'Our people are our greatest assest', drones the average executive at the Annual General Meeting, whilst announcing an inflation-busting pay rise for the board and a pay freeze for the staff. But actually it's true, all other aspects of a business model are replicable in a short space of time, but an ability to really galvanise a workforce puts you alongside the likes of Virgin and Toyota. It is reckoned that the average manager has a team of eight people. If we say that the cost to the organisation of employing each person is about £20,000 then the average manager is presiding over assets of £160,000. It's high time we made sure that we look after these assets properly and ensured managers have the coaching skills to generate the maximum return on such a level of investment.

OK, enough of the soap box. I hope I've convinced you of the need to take up coaching so let's turn our sights to the benefits you'll derive from doing so.

Benefits for the coach

The big prize is improved performance. Both the improved performance of a well-coached team and your own performance as their boss. This is important as increasingly organisations are waking up to the fact that managers ought to be judged on their ability to get results from others. Some go as far as to include measures in these areas in their performance review systems. I think it's very encouraging to see targets concerning coaching and development alongside those for sales and cost containment. It's also crucial for the modern manager to recognise that 'managing' is different to 'doing'. The most obvious example perhaps being in the sales environment when many managers struggle with not being able to get out in the field to sell their wares themselves but have to influence their team to do so instead. Allied to this then is the benefit of saving time. Traditional management positions the manager as being the person with the answers, so if a team member approaches their manager with a problem, he or she will tell them how to solve it. Of course the next time there's a similar problem the same manager will be approached again for the same answer and more time is wasted. If through coaching we help people develop some skills and independence at the same time as solving a problem then soon they are able to solve problems for themselves and managers have more time to do more coaching and build this capability still further.

All of this leads to improved relationships – another key benefit for the coaching manager. Coaching, with its emphasis on asking questions such that people can discover answers for themselves, honours other people's intelligence. We are demonstrating our positive view of their ability and when people are valued in this way they begin to see management and managers in a different light, are more forthcoming in coaching conversations, more willing to show initiative without waiting to be told and thus another helpful loop has been established. Telling and instructing on the other hand fails to tap into other people's abilities, their thinking muscles go into atrophy and they become quite resentful of a situation which finds them simply following orders. A coaching approach will also tap into each individual's internal drivers or motivation and avoid you having to rely on company policy regarding salary and rewards as the only source of motivation. We'll see later on that if these more external sources of motivation are inappropriate they can do more harm than good.

So, to use a cliché, adopting coaching principles will see you able to work *on* your team, rather than *in* your team. As your people become more willing and able to take on matters of task, it frees your time – and your mind – to concentrate on longer term priorities and solving problems once and for all rather than firefighting each time they recur. An ability to do this is a skill highly prized by employers and it's no surprise to see coaching now listed amongst the essential skills required in management job advertisements. Developing an ability to coach will do your career prospects no harm at all.

Benefits for the coachee

The most obvious way in which the people you coach benefit from the coaching you do is in an improved level of performance. If they are sales people, they'll sell more. If they are themselves managers, they'll manage better. If they are administrators, they'll become better at administrating. If they are lecturers they'll deliver more interesting lectures. I can't think of any area of work that won't improve with effective coaching. Of course, if your organisation links such improvements to financial rewards then there's an obvious carrot to dangle. However, as we'll see later on, this may be a rather clumsy approach to motivation and it is helpful to stress some of the other benefits outlined here too.

People who are coached report that they find their work more interesting. This is because coaching makes them curious once more. I once trained as coaches the managers who worked in a factory that made cosmetic components – the brushes and applicators for mascara and so on. 'How can I motivate someone whose job is simply to glue bristles onto make-up brush stems as they trundle pass on a conveyor belt?' I was asked. My advice was to coach around interest and ask the person concerned questions like: 'How could this line be better organised?' 'How could you increase throughput by 10 per cent?' 'How much wastage could be avoided?' To answer such questions, the people being coached had to pay more attention to what they were doing and, as such even the most mundane of tasks became interesting and possibly even fun...

This leads to another benefit, which is increased confidence. The two ingredients to confidence are success and responsibility for that success. Let's say our production line operator finds a way to increase throughput by 10 per cent, and does so entirely on their own initiative. It may seem a small accomplishment in the grand scheme of things but could provide the employee with a real fillip from which we can build. In a similar vein, coaching leads to expanded comfort zones as people realise they're capable of much more.

Try this exercise: From a standing position, go into a squat until you just begin to feel a slight twinge in the thighs. Call this position 1 and hold it for about twenty seconds. Now squat further down until you're thighs hurt a fair bit and it feels quite uncomfortable. Call this position 2 and hold for about ten seconds. Now return to position 1. Doesn't this feel much more comfortable (and a relief!) than the first time? When we try new things and achieve some successes and some learning with the help of a coach, our comfort zones at work expand in much the same way. I am regularly delighted by people I meet on training courses who stutter and mumble their way through the icebreakers only to make interesting and articulate flipchart presentations by the end of the course. It's amazing what we can achieve when supported by people who want to see us succeed.

Benefits for the organisation

All organisations are concerned with performance. Where the profit-making enterprise will concentrate on the bottom line and creating value for its shareholders, the public organisation will need to provide value for the communities it serves, who fund it in one way or another via taxation. Even the 'not for profit' organisation will want to perform, because it is a 'not for loss' organisation too. Coaching improves performance at the organisation level, because organisations are collections of people and if they perform better as individuals and teams so does the organisation as a whole. The bottom line will increase largely as a result of improvement in the top line – turnover and productivity – rather than swingeing cost-cutting exercises.

Organisations that see coaching as a key management skill produce more, but with no loss of quality. Staff who are coached feel more valued and tend to care more about the quality of output they produce. Formal quality methodologies, such as those provided by the International Organisation for Standardisation (ISO) or Investors in People (IiP) are welcomed by employees and not seen with the cynicism that is otherwise often the case. Staff who are coached feel genuinely appreciated and respond in kind.

Many staff will have responsibility for resources – finance, time, equipment, staff of their own and so on. It follows that the organisation will want to see these resources put to good use. Coaching has an emphasis on making people responsible and empowered and organisations that are benefiting from coaching know they can trust their staff to use resources wisely. Take for example an account manager with their own budget for client entertainment. Is there any reason to expect that they will be any less careful with the amount they spend than the executive in charge of the function? Coached properly, they'll exercise as much discretion as the next person. Strangled by expenses claim forms and signing off procedures they'll likely find ways of hiding expenses as a way of 'getting their own back'.

I remember doing some follow-up work in an organisation whose managers we'd trained as coaches and being told, 'You know, coaching makes people think as if this place was their own business'. What a wonderful outcome! One thing that follows this change in thinking is a definite improvement in customer service as employees begin to realise that the customer really is the most vital cog in the whole machine. Once organisations have been established with investors' money, customers become the only real source of revenue and profit. Every other business activity is simply a different way of spending customers' money. Customer facing staff can only treat customers as well as they feel treated themselves. Thus if we treat staff better through coaching they will in turn take more care of the customers.

A coaching organisation will see relationships improve across the whole organisation as people get together and have coaching conversations. Of course there have been conversations at work of one kind or another as long as we've had organisations, but a coaching conversation is different. It is firstly a meeting of equals where the tacit agreement is that anything can be raised and discussed openly and honestly. It is a conversation that looks ahead to what needs to happen next rather than one which dwells on what happened. It is one where every last drop of learning is sought but that also emphasises taking action. In the end, coaching is about doing not talking, but talking means we *do* the right things.

With coaching as the prevailing management style, morale and motivation improves with a consequently dramatic effect on staff retention. Given that the Chartered Institute of Personnel and Development (CIPD) estimates the average cost of an employee leaving at £4,625, this is clearly a significant gain. It has been said that people 'join organisations but leave managers' and there is probably a lot of truth in this. Listen to the conversations in coffee shops and bars where workers gather at lunchtime and take note of their moans and groans. Some will be grumbling about the lack of choice in the staff restaurant or the battle for car-parking, but I'll bet the majority of complaints are about treatment at the hands of management. Of course coaching alone cannot fix otherwise destructive relationships but it does shine a light on where things are going wrong and what may need to change.

So coaching not only helps us retain key people in the organisation but also their skills and attributes. We're constantly being told by the business gurus that we now operate in the knowledge economy, that the days of labouring in exchange for wages and salary are over and that firms live or die by their ability to change, learn and use their core competencies and knowledge. We need to cultivate the knowledge and skill that reside in the workforce, nurture and develop them and ensure it is passed on to the next generation. What better way to do this than through coaching?

There are counter arguments though. Some say that there's no point in hanging on to staff who have reached the top of their salary scale unless you can offer them career advancement which isn't so easy anymore. Others suggest that investing in the development of staff is a waste as they'll probably leave and their next employer gains all the benefit. I believe both these arguments are flawed. There is more to working life than climbing the greasy pole of career advancement and if people are earning enough to fulfil their needs, learning, developing and enjoying themselves, the chances are they'll stay. Some might leave for more money and good luck to them, that's their choice – are they the people you'd want to hang around anyway? Some might leave after you've invested in the training, but that's no reason to withhold development from everyone else. You can always insert a 'payback clause' in any agreement to fund, say, an external qualification.

In coaching conversations regarding people's current situation at work and how they'd like to see that developing, recognise as well that from the organisation's point of view invaluable data for career and succession planning will be captured. Coaching also helps solve the conundrum presented by those who say, 'I'm okay where I am and don't want to progress'. This is not a normal reaction and in my experience has been caused by poor management in the past or external factors getting in the way now. Again, progress does not have to equate to a new job with a promotion; coaching helps people progress in terms of being the best they can be in their current role.

Many of the benefits we've considered until now are available in the short term, but coaching also offers the prospect of building a foundation for new skills development as the organisation embraces learning, making it part of what it means to work there and attracting people with a learning disposition. All of which will make the organisation more competitive as the knowledge and skills needed to operate successfully in a market need constantly to be updated. Some ageing managers may have been able to resist the technological revolution when word processing was all they had to worry about – after all they still had their secretaries to take care of such things – but what about the impact of the Internet and the World Wide Web? Managers and staff at all levels and in all organisations are having to get used to the new business models and ways of working that the Internet has brought about. Teachers cannot afford to be left behind by their pupils. Business leaders cannot afford to be overtaken by two young people on a laptop in a bedroom and we can none of us afford to ignore the opportunities and threats that the digital age presents. But all of this requires an ability to learn at speed. If, as has been suggested, high performers are simply those people (and organisations) that learn quicker, then we are obliged to turn to coaching to make that happen. It follows that coaching also prompts entrepreneurial thinking as it encourages people to think creatively and offers rewards for voicing ideas.

Coaching over the longer term also offers better value from learning and development activity. Classroom training, for example, has been shown to have a much greater effect when the trainee is supported by their 'coach' as they put into practice what they've learnt. Of course there is a time and possibly a monetary cost of putting the coaching in place, but this is a fraction of the amount lost through poorly implemented training or learning that is allowed to wither on the vine. If training budgets are tight, coaching represents the most efficient means of employee development, when perhaps more formal training or courses are not available. When line managers deliver the coaching, their staff are learning and developing every working day, not just at formal training sessions. I mentioned earlier the comment about employees behaving as if the business were their own. What if everyone in the business thought and acted as if they were self-employed? They'd be looking to be the best they can be, they'd be mindful of cost, and constantly alert to new opportunities. Coaching may not foster this spirit everywhere or for all of the time, but it's certain that command and control won't do it at all!

Summary

If there is one fundamental point I would like you to take away from this chapter it's that coaching is about performance. In the world of work, performance comes in many guises: making sales, controlling costs, being inventive, communicating clearly, improving quality, doing things at speed, producing results under pressure, handling customers, working in teams, managing staff... the list goes on and on. Quite simply, people who are coached well by their managers perform better in these areas than those who are not.

From the small business to the large public body, staff costs are likely to be the greatest expense an organisation incurs. It follows that we should want to get the best return on that expenditure we can.

Added to that are a host of other benefits. Communication and relationships improve, motivation increases, good people are inclined to stay longer and those that don't perform so well are encouraged to reach their potential. Coaching provides opportunities for coach and coachee alike to find ways of solving problems and exploiting new opportunities.

INSTANT TIP

Because it is still quite a new discipline, it is likely that you will need senior support in your organisation before coaching can really take off. You will have to make a case for the resources you need. Spend time finding out about the current threats and opportunities your organisation faces and make sure you show how coaching will address them.

03

How do I get people to want to be coached?

Introduction

Why are you reading this book?

Maybe you feel that learning about coaching and therefore improving your management skills will make you more secure in your current job or improve your CV and thus your employment prospects. Perhaps you hope that your new coaching skills will improve your relationships in the team, or it may be that you'd value the kudos that would come from being a coaching manager. It might be that for you, coaching is just a better way to interact with people and you want to see them thrive and you want to give something back. Maybe you were just bored and started flicking through or maybe you were told to read it.

People's rationale for doing things – their motivation – is seldom simple and neither are the variety of models and theories that have been developed to help us understand the nature of motivation in a work setting. They range from the over-simplistic – people move towards pleasure or away from pain – to the extremely complex.

Here is Porter and Lawler's expectancy (or instrumentality) model of motivation:

$$E\ (\text{Effort}) = (E \rightarrow P) \times \sum [(P \rightarrow O) \times V]$$

To expand on this equation:

- **expectancy** – if I tried it could I do it?
- **instrumentality** – if I did it will I attain the required **outcome**?
- **valence** (a subjective value) – do I really value the available **outcomes**?

In the end an appreciation of motivation is developed by understanding what people want from a situation and how they go about achieving such aims. As a manager of people – particularly one interested in using coaching to improve results – an understanding of motivation will contribute greatly to your efforts and help build the necessary flexibility into your approach.

My intention in this chapter is to provide a basis for understanding motivation in general terms firstly and specifically as it relates to coaching later on. I will not subscribe to any one particular theory but set out the most important and enduring models which seem to give us the most clues about the nature of motivation at work. We'll see how approaches to motivation have matured from the rather ham-fisted 'carrot and stick' (yes, yes, I know it still goes on) to the modern-day focus on self-motivation which has its roots in the school of humanistic psychology. You may have a certain scepticism towards applying psychology at work and you're probably right to be cautious, but we'll see how the ideas from the theorists and gurus can be applied in a practical way.

We'll work on the assumption that every employee you coach is unique and that no one theory fits all circumstances. We'll also assume that behaviours influenced by motivation are *choices* and that our people are not just rats trapped in a maze chasing peanuts.

The final two sections of this chapter will pay specific attention to the coaching of 'difficult' people and reluctant coachees. Two instances in which an appreciation of what makes people tick (or dare I say tick better, longer, faster, more cheaply) can provide a real breakthrough.

Motivation classified

I've been involved in the crazy old world of work long enough to realise the massive difference between people performing because they *have* to and people performing because they *want* to. I think in its simplest form then motivation at work is simply the degree to which people *want* to perform. This being the case, motivation for coaching becomes the degree to which people want to do better. It is perfectly possible to make people perform through some kind of mixture of threat or reward, but this is unlikely to produce a sustainable level of performance. It is perfectly possible to deliver coaching to people who do not want it but it is a waste of time and will likely prove counterproductive.

While it's possible to see the usefulness of appreciating motivation as the driving force which propels individuals towards outcomes they want, we can also begin to appreciate the degree of complexity in understanding motivation given the infinite variety of changing, and often conflicting needs and expectations of people at work. In short, different people want different things.

To deal with such complexity we need to break these needs and expectations into categories, for example *extrinsic* and *intrinsic* motivation. Extrinsic motivation is related to tangible rewards such as salary and bonuses, security, advancement and conditions of employment. I'm guessing most of you reading this will have little or no influence over such rewards, but will certainly be aware of your team's feelings towards them. Intrinsic motivation refers to psychological rewards like pride, satisfaction, opportunity and recognition. These you most certainly can influence as a coach, particularly when you are the line manager too.

Another way to consider classifying motivation is to consider the orientation people take towards work: what are the things that most concern or interest them? Some people take what's known as an *instrumental* orientation to work and are concerned with 'other things'. Such people will be most interested in economic rewards such as pay and pension arrangements. Other people take a *personal* orientation – they are concerned with 'themselves'. These people are most likely to be concerned by intrinsic motivators such as satisfaction and personal growth. Finally we find groups of people who take a *relational* orientation to work, concerning 'other people'. They are concerned with relationships, friendships, status and belonging.

It may also be useful to classify the reactions people have to *not* getting what they want at or from work. You'll see people respond to these circumstances in a constructive way by solving the inherent problem or adjusting their needs and expectations. You'll also see people responding in a negative way by, for example, becoming aggressive to colleagues and others, by withdrawing and becoming sulky or by giving up completely – in spirit if not in body.

Later we'll see how coaching creates awareness of the reasons behind these responses and encourages employees to take responsibility for accessing their motivation in a helpful and positive way.

Key research

Let's now turn our sights on the key researchers and see how their findings can contribute to our being able to increase motivation through coaching and increase the motivation to be coached.

Frederick W. Taylor (1856–1915): scientific management

Taylor was an American engineer who achieved his qualifications the hard way, via evening studies. From humble beginnings as an engineer in a steel company he became one of the most influential management writers and theorists. He is best known for defining the techniques of *scientific management* which is the study of the relationship between people and tasks for the purpose of redesigning work processes to increase efficiency.

He wrote at a time when the growing complexity of factories was creating big management problems. Taylor was one of the first to attempt to systematically analyse behaviour at work. He likened the organisation to a machine and his methods involved breaking each task down to its smallest unit to identify the best way to do each job. Next the supervisor would teach it to the worker and make sure the worker did only those actions essential to the task. Hence *scientific management* as Taylor attempted to make a science for each element and remove human variability or errors. Taylor believed that by increasing specialisation, the production process would become more efficient.

Taylor's steps began with studying the way workers performed their tasks, gathering all the informal job knowledge they possessed, and experimenting with ways of improving task performance to increase efficiency. Any resulting new methods of performing tasks were written into work rules and standard operating procedures. He also advocated carefully selecting workers that possessed the skills and abilities needed for the task and training them to perform the tasks according to these rules and procedures. The next suggested step was to establish a fair or acceptable level of performance for a task and then develop a pay system that provides a higher reward for performance above the acceptable level. Finally he proposed splitting the task of the first-line supervisor into eight specialist positions with each held by a different person, an idea which may have led to the notion of *matrix management*.

His ideas had a major effect on organisation of work and the way people were managed. Unfortunately, although things became more productive they also became repetitive and monotonous and many employees became very unhappy at work. Initially productivity under Taylor's methods dramatically increased and it seemed to work. New departments appeared, such as personnel and quality control. More and more middle managers appeared as planning was separated from operations. Formality was increased and the supervisor with stopwatch and clipboard appeared in all work settings which workers found all kinds of ways to resist.

No doubt you can see that much of scientific management remains with us today, but the efficiencies it brought have mostly disappeared. The problem is the machine metaphor. People aren't parts in a machine, but living, breathing human beings who these days have a variety of wants and needs that they wish their work to fulfil. Positioning coaching as merely a means to increased efficiency, whatever the economic rewards that follow, is unlikely to create more than a short-term spike in performance overall.

Elton Mayo (1880–1949): the Hawthorne experiments

Perhaps the most famous experiments in motivation took place at the Western Electric Company's Hawthorne plant in Chicago. Between 1924 and 1932, five sets of tests were carried out in an attempt to understand what made workers assembling telephone equipment more productive.

To begin with the experiments concentrated on improvements to lighting. Productivity indeed improved, but it also improved when the lights were dimmed. This odd result was repeated in experiments which looked at pay, incentives, rest periods, hours of work, and supervision. Mayo advanced two theories.

He firstly suggested that the very fact of being involved in an experiment encouraged the workers to be more productive. It created interest and involvement in their repetitive work, and their managers began taking an interest in how they felt. Mayo's second theory was that social interaction had a critical effect on motivation because the experiment meant bringing workers together in teams with a positive relationship with a supervisor.

In any event, it seemed the workers simply appreciated the change the experiments brought about, felt more valued and generally happier and thus their performance improved.

Mayo's research has come in for much criticism over the years, with many claiming that it was the incentives that the workers were offered to participate that actually caused the increase in productivity. Nevertheless his studies shifted the science of management from Taylor's engineering approach to a *social sciences approach*. Almost at once, management became a question of considering motivation, leadership and group dynamics. The human relations approach was born. Managers still had to design jobs, select and train the employees and create a reward structure, but were now also responsible for leading, motivating, communicating and generally monitoring the social setting in which work took place. There was a change from task focus to people focus, which even today many managers find difficult to make.

Had we understood coaching better at the time of the Hawthorne experiments, the transition from scientific management would have been easier to make, for coaching is concerned with both tasks and people. It is performance focused, with an intent to take action, make changes and create mobility, but is also person centred in recognising that – in the end – it is people that take action, make changes and become mobile. Creating an appetite for coaching requires us to stress the potential for finding out about oneself as well as finding ways to improve the way that work is carried out.

The phenomenon uncovered by Mayo's experiments has since been labelled the *Hawthorne effect*. It has become the scourge of researchers who would prefer to be able to isolate or ignore its effects and explains why much modern research into Human Resource Development (HRD) studiously ignores words such as 'proof', 'fact' and 'cause'. But the Hawthorne effect can be a boon to managers that coach who – provided their intentions are sincere – can be assured that simply taking a keen interest in the human side of business and work will create a more positive climate and provide the basis for improved results.

Douglas McGregor (1906–1964): Theory X and Theory Y

Douglas McGregor was an American social psychologist. In his book *The Human Side of Enterprise* (McGraw Hill, 1960) he proposed that there are two distinct schools of thought when it comes to employee behaviour. He called these presuppositions Theory X and Theory Y.

Theory X

The average employee...

- dislikes work
- avoids responsibility
- responds to threats
- needs close control.

Theory Y

The average employee...

- welcomes work
- seeks responsibility
- responds to problems
- is self-motivated.

In short, managers subscribing to Theory X are very task-oriented and managers who subscribe to Theory Y are very people-oriented. It is important to recognise that McGregor did not suggest that either of these theories was valid in itself. In practice, most managers' attitudes and behaviour are a mixture of X and Y, with Y predominating unless external pressures and demands move them towards X. Few people these days would subscribe to Theory X as a matter of general principle and it does not seem to agree with the research on people's attitudes towards work. However, Theory Y can present problems as some work really does require close supervision and control and the level of responsibility individuals are prepared to accept does vary. As a general rule though a people-oriented approach more closely reflects employees' aspirations and motivations and thus can create a very helpful self-fulfilling prophecy, as the following story illustrates.

The boards of two fiercely competitive companies decided to organise a rowing match to challenge each other's organisational and sporting abilities. The first company was strongly Theory X: ruthless, autocratic, no staff empowerment, etc. The second company was more Theory Y: a culture of developing people, devolved responsibility and decision-making.

On the day of the race, The Y company's boat appeared from the boathouse first, its crew comprising eight rowers and a single helmsman (the cox). Then came the X company boat, with its crew comprising eight helmsmen and just a single rower.

Happily, for those of us who hold of positive view of people at work, the Y company's boat won easily.

The following day the X company board of directors held an inquest with the crew, to review what had been learned from the embarrassing defeat, which might be of benefit to the organisation as a whole, and any future re-match.

After a long and tiring meeting the X company board finally reached a conclusion. They decided that the rower should be replaced immediately because clearly he had not listened well enough to the instructions he'd been given!

McGregor's message for managers who coach is clear. Before we sit down and hold coaching conversations, we must challenge the assumptions we hold about people. If we choose to make Theory Y assumptions about the attitudes and motivations of people and treat them accordingly, they will start to behave as if the theory is true.

Abraham Maslow (1908–1970): the hierarchy of needs

Maslow's hierarchy of needs was developed between 1943 and 1954 and first published in *Motivation and Personality* in 1954.

According to his original model there are five kinds of need that are common to us all, and these five needs are typically arranged on a pyramid (see Figure 3.1).

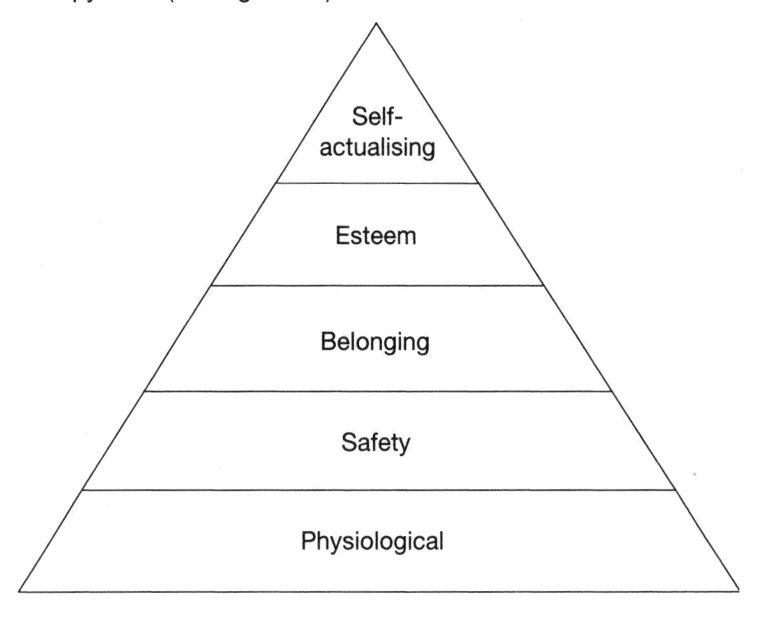

Figure 1.1: Maslow's hierarchy of needs

Physiological needs refer to the very basics: air, water, food, sleep and shelter. These needs are met mostly outside of work, but since our society requires us to use money to provide for these needs, they are represented in the workplace by basic pay and conditions. In simple terms, if someone is too cold, the motivation to find warmth is likely to override all other objectives.

The need for safety drives us to find secure environments and again one would hope that this would be a given in the modern world of work for most people. Safety needs at work therefore become a matter of seeking assurance that our basic, physiological needs will be met in the future. Output and performance can fall dramatically following rumours of a take-over or merger, for example. Few organisations are still able to offer the 'job for life' that used to be commonplace, but good training and development that builds employability and good clear communication about any proposed changes likely to affect financial safety and security will go a long way to satisfying these needs.

Belonging needs occur because we are social animals that form social groups naturally. Unless individuals feel they belong to a certain group, the objectives of that group are almost irrelevant. Outside of work people fulfil their need for belonging through family, friends, sports and social activities, and so on. Within work it is important to make sure everybody feels a part of the working group, hence the popularity of team-building events and away days. Our belonging needs also cover the feeling of needing to be needed. We all want to feel as if we have a useful contribution to make to the team.

At the next level we can satisfy our need for self-esteem by achieving a certain mastery over the tasks that we undertake, being good at what we do in other words. Our need to feel the esteem of others drives us towards feeling a sense of status, which can often be met through job titles and the 'perks' that go with reaching a certain level in an organisation.

Self-actualising is when we feel confident enough to pursue individual goals. People who reach this level turn their sights to making a contribution and on doing a job that is meaningful, that makes a difference.

The main lessons we can learn from Maslow are that a fulfilled need no longer motivates and that people can move down the hierarchy as well as up. This helps us recognise that motivation is dynamic and that we need ongoing coaching conversations with our people to understand how their needs and consequently their motivation changes.

Frederick Herzberg (1923–2000): two factor theory

Imagine that we went back in time to the moment of your birth. Imagine that from the second that you entered the world, you were raised in a totally controlled physical environment. Imagine if every aspect of life within your plastic bubble was controlled from outside. You were fed and nourished, kept clean and healthy, given carefully controlled exposure to bugs and diseases so that you could build up immunity, made to undertake physical exercise, and so on. When you reached adulthood would you be well?

Probably not. You would likely be okay physically, but emotionally and spiritually you'd be a wreck. In the absence of any emotional attachments, exposure to nature, a chance to love and be loved you would not become a rounded, mature human being at all. At best you would be 'not ill', but this is of course a very different state to being well.

Herzberg's *two factor theory* recognises a similar situation when considering workplace motivation, in that between highly motivated and completely dissatisfied there is 'not demotivated'. A strange condition perhaps, but also a surprisingly common one.

In his investigation of two hundred accountants in the USA, Herzberg found that motivation and satisfaction were influenced by the components of two factors. The first group of components are called the hygiene factors. They include working conditions, quality of supervision, salary, status, security and organisation policies and administration. Herzberg determined that these factors need to be seen as appropriate to ensure an employee does not become dissatisfied but do not lead to high levels of motivation. In simple terms, they get us to 'not demotivated'. The second group, the motivation factors, include achievement, recognition, responsibility, job interest and personal growth. These factors were seen as conducive to real motivation.

Herzberg's work supports Maslow's hierarchy of needs. The major influencers of motivation or dissatisfaction are closely linked to status or esteem in Maslow's words and this fits the profile of modern organisations where physiological needs and needs relating to belonging and safety will have been met. This is perhaps best understood in relation to pay or salary. Levels of pay are rarely viewed in terms of their contribution to basic needs, but more commonly as a status measure. In other words, it's not the amount of pay in absolute terms that's the issue, but relative pay as an indication of status and as a contributor to esteem.

The best advice for the coaching manager seems to be to try to appeal to the motivation factors, even where there is dissatisfaction with the hygiene factors, otherwise we might as well give up before we start. Use coaching to recognise achievement, generate responsibility, and encourage personal development. The hygiene factors are probably outside your area of influence anyway, unless you happen to be a senior decision maker, but a focus on the motivation factors can lessen the effect of any dissatisfaction with the hygiene factors.

Let's now look at what we can learn from the theorists and apply it to a couple of tricky coaching situations.

Coaching 'reluctant' people

Why would anyone be reluctant to work in a coaching relationship when, as we've seen, it's all about helping them to access their ability and achieve success?

Once people get to know you as a manager who coaches, you can expect a steady stream of motivated, intelligent, ambitious individuals to beat a path to your door. I think it fair to warn you that they'll not just be from your own reporting line or department either. These people are likely to be performing well already, but will want to do even better.

So far so good, but what about the people you want to coach who aren't clamouring for your attention? What about the people you're going to have to coach and help improve before more serious procedures are brought to bear? This requires more thought.

Some will be reluctant to be coached simply because they are nervous about what to expect or are simply misinformed. Coaching has been misrepresented in certain circles and some unhelpful myths have emerged. Some see coaching as purely remedial and undertaking coaching therefore as some kind of admission of weakness. Others have seen the popular media latch on to the worst of the life coaching movement and may fear that you'll have them pretending to be a tree in search of spiritual enlightenment. None of this could be further from the truth. The antidote to such misinformation is good quality information and I would recommend that before any coaching conversations commence you take time to explore what the person concerned understands about coaching to allay any fears and clear up any misunderstandings. The section on what coaching is and what it isn't in Chapter 1 will help.

Others will be reluctant because coaching really is remedial in their situation and has perhaps been arranged as part of an overall attempt at managing the recovery of a genuine poor performer. It may even be the precursor to invoking the organisation's disciplinary procedure. This is far from the ideal backdrop to successful coaching and if you're being asked to be a third party coach (i.e. coach to someone other than a member of your own team) then you need to be careful that the line manager concerned is not just abdicating responsibility because they cannot tackle poor performance. Trust will be the single most important element in the coaching relationship that you forge and I recommend a largely informal first meeting where you and the coachee can each establish a few ground rules. I also think such a meeting should look at identifying a few strengths as people in these situations can often feel a bit weather beaten and as if everyone is against them. This is not a soft approach – it is absolutely necessary to restore some self-belief if there's to be any chance of recovery. Next you can establish some arrangements to include things like time schedule and confidentiality, and I always find it useful to set some coaching objectives – to define, if you like, what success will look like. It should then be possible to get into detailed coaching in later sessions with many of the barriers removed.

Coaching 'difficult' people

In the first instance, look for the cause. We don't generally recruit known cynics or troublemakers, so if someone is proving to be a difficult employee the first step might be to understand what has happened in their past to cause this behaviour.

Deal with performance not person. A great trick if you can pull it off (and not easy in emotional situations) is to try to deal with what the person *does* rather than get tangled up in the sort of person they *are*. This means that when offering feedback – often a necessary step before the real coaching can begin – limit your observations to what actually happened and the consequences rather than judging things as good, bad or otherwise. People can't argue with the facts, but they can argue against your judgements. Similarly, try to avoid commenting on attitude. Attitude must be the most subjective term used at work. Every one of us believes that our own attitude is useful and appropriate or we would change it, so telling someone they have the wrong attitude is pointless. Describing what they did and the results that ensued will prove much more productive.

When problems arise in the team, deal with them while they're small. If someone does something that irritates you or upsets the team, the time to tackle it is there and then. In fairness, people often don't realise the effects of their actions and unless we point things out, the unhelpful behaviour takes root. Avoid taking sides and if a member of your team asks you to deal with a problem with another member of staff, say that you'll look into it and get back to them. Don't agree that 'X is a real problem and we need to straighten him out'. This could come back to haunt you later on, and besides you'll gain more respect from everyone by your professional approach.

Deal with things in private. At some stage you and your difficult employee are going to need to have a conversation. This must absolutely be done in private if you're to have any chance of getting back on an even keel. But consider the wider team. As Mr Spock used to say in *Star Trek*, 'The needs of the many outweigh the needs of the few and of the one.' When we have difficulties with one member of staff it can be easy for them to soak up all our energy and attention and neglect our other team members.

There's no point placing the problem person in some half-baked project role or inventing some other non-job to get them out of the way: what message does this send? And finally, be prepared to cut your losses. Robert Holden, pioneer in the field of positive psychology, says that 'it's awful when people quit and go, but it's worse when they quit and stay!' If somebody really refuses to change their ways despite your best efforts, it may be better for both parties to go their separate ways.

Summary

In this section we've blended some classic motivation theory with some honest, practical advice on increasing the take-up of coaching. In the end no general view of motivation can replace the value of sitting down with your people and understanding their specific wants and needs – the Instant Tip below starts with this in mind.

F.W. Taylor, widely regarded as the father of scientific management, said that if management would only show the workers how to do the job better and then share rewards of a better job there would be no problem. He argued that management never do this, however, for fear of driving up wages, and so end up lost in a never ending search for 'something for nothing'.

But the challenge of the world of work today means even the most enlightened management would be unable to act on Taylor's advice because management have no more idea on how to do the job better than the person doing it! No wonder the take-up of coaching is increasing at such pace.

The Instant Tip that follows requires you to make a questionnaire for each member of your team. You may need to explain that you're looking at ways to improve motivation and that the starting point is getting a better idea of what makes them tick.

You can get people to put their names on the sheets if you like or you can do it anonymously if you think you'll get a more honest response. If you think issuing questionnaires is a bit heavy handed, pop the questions on a flip chart or white board and have an open team discussion around them. In any event you'll be gathering valuable information about levels and types of motivation in the team which you can use to develop a long-term approach.

INSTANT TIP

If you want to see an immediate boost in levels of motivation, jump on your PC and create a quick questionnaire for each of your team members which asks:

- What aspect of your job do you most enjoy?
- What aspect of your job do you least enjoy?
- What aspect of your job would you like to stay the same?

04

How do I actually coach?

Introduction

We now need to take the themes of the previous sections and examine how the requisite interpersonal skills can be applied within a simple and practical framework. As we've seen, coaching is essentially a one-to-one activity, and managers usually coach their juniors, although they might also coach whole teams, peer groups and even themselves. Managers are seen as good potential coaches because of their experience and expertise. However, just as in sport, it is not necessary for the coach to have better technical skills than the learner. In fact, it can be a serious disadvantage. What is essential is a range of interpersonal skills including good listening, questioning and feedback skills, and the ability to encourage people to think for themselves. The manager also needs an understanding of different learning and personality styles, the ability to build rapport, and self-awareness.

Many of you will be familiar with the widely used GROW model as a means of channelling these sorts of skills and qualities into an effective coaching session. The framework provides a simple four-step structure for a coaching session. During the first step of the session (Goal), coach and coachee agree on a specific topic and objective for the discussion. During the second step (Reality), both coach and coachee invite self-assessment and offer specific examples to illustrate their points. They then move into the third step (Options) where suggestions are offered and choices made. And finally (Will), the coach and coachee commit to action, define a timeframe for their objectives and identify how to overcome possible obstacles.

For my book *Coaching at Work* (John Wiley & Sons, 2006) I replaced GROW with ARROW – with Aims instead of Goals and a Reflection stage after Reality – because I sensed many coaches were using GROW on auto-pilot and I wanted to be sure my readers would think about the model. I will use the ARROW model again here.

A	Aims
R	Reality
R	Reflection
O	Options
W	Way Forward

However, both these models – and any of the many others – are simply mnemonics. They are not cure alls, and neither are they the be all and end all of coaching. The use of GROW or ARROW without the context of raising awareness, generating responsibility and building trust has little value and coaching in this way may cause more problems than it solves. All coaching frameworks must be used in context. Indeed, in research carried out by The Work Foundation (formerly the Industrial Society, a not-for-profit organisation that aims to improve quality in working life) the key components of coaching training programmes were cited as active listening (80%), questioning (75%), providing actionable feedback (72%) and facilitating (63%).

Christopher Orpen, Reader in Management at Bournemouth University, provides further advice on applying the skills and frameworks discussed up to this point:

> *Coaches should:*
>
> - *coach on a regular, not annual basis*
> - *recognise how their own management might be affecting the situation*
> - *provide alternative examples when coaching*
> - *focus on behaviours, not attributes*
> - *use positive reinforcement wherever possible*
> - *not coach too closely.*
>
> Christopher Orpen, 'The Coaching Role of Management' (*Training and Development*, 1994)

All this makes it difficult to see how the skills and competencies of coaching might be taught in the traditional sense or absorbed from the pages of a book like this. In fact the whole idea of teaching coaching is a contradiction in terms, and it's generally people who have been coached well that most readily become good coaches themselves. Therefore, to pass on the necessary skills, the principle must be: you don't teach coaching – you coach it.

So, I will present here a range of ideas, concepts and techniques that will set you along the right path. Please do not view these as a recipe or a set of instructions on the only way to coach. Use them to forge your own style, create your own frameworks, and develop an approach to coaching that fits your organisation. Furthermore, rather than pouring over this section again and again in an effort to get it right, get out there and try some coaching with people who are willing to help you learn and who you trust will give you honest constructive feedback.

Ask questions

The main point to clarify here is that coaches do not ask questions to get answers. Instead they ask questions so that the coachee has to think before providing their response. If everything we do is preceded by thought, then it follows that if we increase the quality of thinking then we'll increase the quality of action or decision.

Asking questions encourages thinking and recognises that the people whom we coach have ideas and input and more importantly, demonstrates that those ideas are welcomed and people's input valued. Telling or instructing does none of these things: it stifles creativity and innovation and encourages a culture of dependency on the manager, with staff seeing them as the person with all the answers. If you've ever found yourself saying (or thinking), 'How many times must I tell you?' or 'If I've told you once, I've told you a thousand times!' you'll know this to be true.

Asking questions will mean that coachees achieve a much greater level of understanding about the work they do and the tasks they complete. You can ask questions in advance of the task to encourage the coachee to think about how they might go about things and the obstacles they might encounter, or you can ask questions after the task to find out what went well or badly, what was learnt and what could be done differently next time. Of course this will demand an investment of time up front from the coach – time that won't always be available – but like any sound investment there will be a significant pay back over time. As the people you coach become more capable and confident because they're thinking so well, they'll become less reliant on you to solve problems and give direction. Where the coachee's work involves repetition, a coaching style that makes good use of thought-provoking questions can save hours of going over the same ground and repeating the same instructions.

Asking questions will promote a level of learning unavailable from the more controlling, 'tell and instruct' approach. Kolb's learning cycle suggests that learning occurs once we've *planned* an experience, had the experience, reflected on the experience and drawn conclusions from the experience (see David Kolb, *Experiential Learning*, Prentice Hall 1985). In the frenetic world of work these days we mostly just plan and do (and sometimes the planning bit gets missed!). A few judicious coaching questions will ensure we reflect and conclude without needing more formal arrangements to do so. All of this is going to lead to a much more involved and therefore motivated employee and so most importantly of all will promote a much higher quality of task completion which can be measured and quantified in terms of money spent or saved, should you wish to prove coaching's worth.

Using the ARROW model

Over the next five sections we'll examine the steps that make up the coaching ARROW questioning sequence. We'll see how these questions promote high-quality thinking and I'll point out some questioning tips and some pitfalls to avoid.

Establish *Aims*

Before you start your conversation by establishing Aims you'll need to establish the situation or problem for discussion. Then you can ask:

In relation to your issue:

- What are you trying to achieve long term?
- How much personal influence do you have over that?
- What first steps could you take?
- Are they challenging but achievable?
- How will you know if you've succeeded?
- What timeframe is involved?

Remember that you are not asking these questions to find out the answers, you're asking them to encourage the coachee to think, at this stage, about the future – how the situation will be when a problem has been solved, a skill developed, a chance taken or whatever.

It's important to recognise that a coaching session must not turn into an interrogation. Use these coaching questions to start a dialogue, but don't feel you have to use them all, or in the same order they appear here. It is also useful if you can develop your own way of asking the same sorts of questions, so that they sound more like you.

There has been a lot of debate in the coaching field about the wisdom of starting a coaching conversation by establishing aims or goals. Some argue that it is not possible to think clearly about a *desired state* before exploring how things stand at the present time. I disagree because I feel that by establishing Aims at the outset we are putting a beacon in place that the coachee can move towards during and after the coaching session. My experience suggests that people make better decisions and wiser choices when they are clear about what they are trying to achieve and why.

Asking these Aims questions also enables the coachee to become clear about the different types of Aim they may be thinking about and how they interrelate as shown in the following table.

dreams	why?	the inspiration
performance goals	what?	the specification
processes	how?	the mechanism

I use the word 'dream' to describe any aim which lacks detail. 'To be the best widget manufacturer in the world' is a dream-level Aim, but so is 'I wish I was more confident'. It doesn't always have to be something grand, just the rationale for wanting to improve things or move forward in the first place. Setting performance goals puts detail on the dream, such as 'to have 35 per cent of the widget market with a gross margin of 10 per cent' or, 'to be fully confident in speaking at the AGM by next June'.

It is important to have all three levels clear in our minds if our goals are to be achieved. The Aims questions provide clarity around dreams and performance goals and the Way Forward questions that come at the end of the coaching ARROW finalise the process steps.

Other useful questions you can experiment with at the Aims stage include:

- What would need to happen in this session for you to consider it time well spent?
- What would you like to be different when you leave this session?
- What would you like to happen that is not happening now?
- How can you communicate your Aims in a compelling way?

Check *Reality*

Having established a specific, clear and measurable Aim, we can now turn our sights to working with our coachees to develop a detailed understanding of their starting point – the current Reality in other words. This is a vital step in the coaching process as it helps coachees become sensitised to what is going on around them and the feelings it invokes. Most of us work for a lot of the time in an almost 'auto pilot' mode where our thinking becomes sluggish and we miss important opportunities to do things better.

Consider these questions:

- What's happening now?
- How much/How often is that happening?

- How does this make you feel?
- Who else is involved?
- What happens to them?
- What have you tried so far?
- What results did you get?

The intention of these questions is to encourage the coachee to live in the 'here and now' or 'in the moment' as it is only in the present that we can make changes.

We need to be mindful of the temptation at the Reality stage of slipping into old 'tell and instruct' habits. If ever you find yourself thinking along the following lines, you may have fallen into a common trap:

'I know exactly how you feel.'

No you don't. You only know how you felt in a similar situation. If I'm having an experience, then that experience is unique. It may appear almost identical to a situation you've experienced, but there will be differences, however subtle. Even if our two situations were exactly alike in every detail, I'm me and you're you. I have fashioned my own model of the world from my own unique experiences and you have done likewise. Our two models cannot possibly be the same. Besides which, does telling me about *your* similar situation and how *you* felt, help *me* move forward?

'No, you're wrong.'

I may look at a set of circumstances and see things differently from you and it may be impossible to determine which of us is right or wrong. Is the glass half full or half empty? It's all a matter of perspective. One of the greatest assets you can utilise as a coach is curiosity. The next time a coachee describes a situation and you disagree try asking, 'How have you reached that conclusion?', 'What evidence do you have for that?' or questions that similarly invite the coachee to really examine things.

'Right, let's move on.'

The final trap is moving on from Reality too quickly. There's real insight to be gained in this part of the questioning sequence but it might need some time.

Other useful questions you can try at the Reality stage include:

- How do you know your perception is accurate?
- What do you think in that situation?
- What do you feel in that situation?
- What other factors are relevant?
- Who else is relevant?
- What is their perception of the situation?

Take time for *Reflection*

We have now reached a point where, in your conversation with your coachee, the two of you have worked together to articulate some aims and explore the starting point – the Reality. You're at a point in the coaching session where it would be appropriate to pause and take a moment or two to think about what's been discovered or reinforced before moving on.

Have a look at these questions:

- How big is the gap between Aims and Reality?
- How realistic are your Ams?
- How certain are you about the Reality of the situation?
- How could you find out more?
- What assumptions are you making?
- Have you been totally honest with yourself?
- What's *really* going on?

It might be that now we've considered Reality, that the Aims look over-optimistic. We could revisit the Aims and consider lengthening the time frame and perhaps putting some short-term performance goals in place to provide some momentum.

On the other hand, it may be that we are working from very limited information about current Reality and are dealing with a whole set of assumptions. In such a case it would be wise to consider stopping the coaching session at that point to make some further enquiries. Take for example the situation of a coachee that tells you management doesn't support new ideas in answer to the question, 'What's happening now?' It might be that historically management haven't supported ideas, but is it the same management team now as it was then? Even if it is, people and circumstances can change.

Asking what's really going on can be a powerful way of uncovering true coaching issues where you sense that the coaching may only be answering the questions superficially. It's a powerful question so use it carefully and sparingly but it can take the conversation to a much more productive level.

In some ways putting Reflection between Reality and Options was done purely for my convenience – to help spell ARROW! Whilst it is useful to spend time on Reflection at that stage, it can be equally useful to make reflecting and reviewing a part of navigating through the whole ARROW sequence. It may be useful to think of the sequence as a series of loops rather than a fixed linear sequence. We may want to ask our coaching questions in a fixed order but you can be certain that your coachee's thinking patterns won't be so rigid and you'll need to be prepared to jump ahead to Way Forward or return to Aims or to move flexibly in and out of the sequence as required.

Here are some more suggestions for thought-provoking, reflective questions:

- What do you believe to be *true*?
- What information are you missing?

- What could you learn from others who have done this?
- Where could you get more information?
- What are the risks?
- What are you scared of?

Generate *Options*

Imagine a large pile of sand and gravel in the middle of the room. Imagine I came along and poured water or some other liquid on the top. The liquid would form small rivulets and run down the sides. If I poured more liquid on the top some more rivulets would be formed but most of the liquid would run into the existing grooves. If I kept doing this – and if the pile didn't collapse – eventually the liquid would only flow in the existing grooves and rivulets and no new grooves would form at all. Things would literally get stuck in a rut. I see the same thing happening in business all the time. People's thinking gets stuck. The same problems recur and we can only think of the same tired old solutions to try in response; even though we often instinctively know they still won't work.

We coaching managers owe it to our people to help lift their thinking out of these ruts.

Consider these questions:

- What could you do about all this?
- What else could you try?
- What if you had more/less (e.g. time, money, status...?)
- Whose advice could you seek?
- What suggestions would they have?
- What would you do if you knew you couldn't fail?
- Would you like another suggestion?

Some of these questions seem a little odd on the face of it, and you may get some frowns and other odd looks in response, but remember the purpose here is to generate fresh thinking. The first time you ask, 'What could you do about all this?' you'll likely get a hackneyed response. That's why we need, 'What else could you try?' (or similar). I've often found it useful to ask this question perhaps as much as half a dozen times to really encourage my coachees to dig deep and find a fresh idea. It's hard work but the results tend to be worth it. Asking the question repeatedly also offers a number of chances for the coachee to suggest the thing they intuitively know they ought to be suggesting, but are hesitating over for some reason. Encourage a feeling of looking for quantity rather than quality of answers at this stage. There's time to evaluate and question the viability of options later on at the Way Forward stage, but doing this too soon tends to discourage creative thinking.

The main pitfall at the Options stage is the temptation to add your own suggestions too soon. It's perfectly OK to offer your own ideas but not before the coachee has been given every opportunity to come up with lots of their own ideas. There's also the chance that your ideas will be seen as better simply because you're the boss and there's a built-in excuse if they don't work out or things go wrong!

Here are a few more examples, but do try to think of some of your own as well:

- What actions have you already considered?
- Who else could you involve?
- What advice would you give a friend in your situation?
- Which options do you like the most?

Establish the *Way Forward*

So we've created a destination point by establishing some Aims, we understand the extent of the journey because we've taken time to understand the current Reality, and a pause for Reflection has enabled us to clarify our thinking and understanding. We've generated a number of Options and now it's simply a question of deciding which option to choose, right? Wrong.

Deciding which option to choose is pointless unless we actually *take action*. It's like deciding to move to a nicer area but never phoning an estate agent, or deciding to get fitter without changing our diet or exercise habits. Thought without action is just an idle dream.

This then is the point of the Way Forward section. Our intention at this stage is to turn thought into action. The following questions will help:

- What exactly are you going to do?
- When exactly are you going to do it?
- Who needs to know?
- How and when will you tell them?
- What resources do you need?
- How will you get them?
- Will this take you towards your aims?
- What do you need me to do?
- What is your commitment to this course of action on a scale of 1–10?

You'll need to be quite tough but encouraging at this stage as human nature seems to get us quite attached to the status quo, even when our current situation is causing problems and anxiety. The point of using the word 'exactly' in the first two questions is to encourage coachees to articulate detailed action steps, making a commitment to themselves first. Sometimes, you might need to hold your tongue if you feel that an action step described at the Way Forward stage is over-optimistic or just plain wrong. Sometimes it might be better to let your coachee try and fail. At least they are moving and at least they will learn from the experience. Of course, if an action step is against the organisation's rules, illegal, harmful or unsafe, you'll need to intervene, but you can at least explain to the coachee why a certain plan may not be possible. It's these sorts of judgements that make coaching an art form and a skill and so much more than just reeling off a list of questions which any fool could do.

The final commitment question is a good way of clarifying the extent to which our coaching has been successful. A response of less than 10 can be followed by, 'What would you have to change to make it a 10' to throw light on where any blockages may still remain. Other useful questions include:

- What's the best thing you could be thinking to get what you want?
- What's the best thing you could be feeling to get what you want?
- What could you delegate?
- What could you start today?
- What do you gain/lose by this action?
- What have you learnt today?

Observe

So, we're asking carefully constructed coaching questions and listening intently to the response. You can also gain a lot of feedback about how well the session is progressing and the coachee's readiness for change by monitoring their non-verbal communication – that is their tone of voice and body language.

Professor Albert Mehrabian's famous statistics back this up:

- 7 per cent of meaning is in the words that are spoken
- 38 per cent of meaning is paralinguistic (the way that the words are said)
- 55 per cent of meaning is in body language.

These statistics often seem odd at first glance, but they do make sense. Certainly words alone can be very confusing. Consider for example this sign that I saw on a recent trip on the London Underground system.

Dogs must be carried on the escalator

Simple enough sign, but I looked at it and thought, 'What if you haven't got a dog?' My business brain got ticking and I began to think there might be an opportunity to rent dogs to commuters that they could carry on the escalator and hand in at the top. Someone from the dog rental firm would have to re-stock say every half hour by bringing a big basket full of dogs back down to the beginning. How easily we can get side-tracked by unclear communication!

The power of paralinguistic communication – tone of voice – has been well known to politicians and those in the public eye for years. Just watch as any politician comes to prominence and you can almost see the work of the voice coaches coming through.

Body language consists of four elements:

- **Posture** – how we hold ourselves whilst standing or sitting
- **Gestures** – the way we use our hands
- **Expression** – our eye, brow and mouth movements
- **Adornment** – the use of make-up, tattoos, jewellery and so on.

The good coach will monitor body language and tone of voice to check that these things are in sync with what the coachee is saying. If, for example, the coachee is claiming to be committed to the latest change project whilst slouched in their chair yawning, it's clear what the real message is. Be wary though of seeing too much in signals. Scratching my nose may well mean I'm lying, but could also mean I have an itchy nose. Folding my arms may well be a defensive gesture or it could simply mean I'm more comfortable that way. It is groups of signals that give the real message, not single gestures.

As well as monitoring the coachee's non-verbal communication, you can also use your own to help the conversation flow. Three ideas from Neuro-Linguistic Programming (NLP) are particularly helpful:

- **Pacing** – matching the coachee's speed and volume of speech.
- **Mirroring** – matching the body language of the coachee (carefully and subtly though I would suggest).
- **Leading** – changing your own non-verbal communication and bring the coachee with you.

Listen

I'll assume here that your hearing is not impaired in any physical way and that your listening faculties are basically intact. How well do you listen? When people talk to you at work do you become oblivious to everything else or do you still partly monitor other conversations or watch what else is happening. Do you patiently wait while the speaker rummages in their mind for just the right word to describe their thoughts or do you finish their sentence for them, impatient to move on?

Listening is without doubt the key skill of the effective coach. In fact, it is the key skill of any professional engaged in helping others, from marriage guidance counsellor to careers adviser. It is however a skill often deployed quite poorly because it is confused with hearing, which we do all the time, and not recognised as a skill which needs attention and practice. This problem is exacerbated by the fact that when we talk of listening we are not talking about one thing. There are three levels of listening.

- **Level One** listening is superficial. We hear the words of the other person, but the focus is on what it means to us.

This brings about the problem we saw earlier that happens at the Reality stage of the ARROW questioning sequence. Namely that we worry about forming our own reality as coach, rather than allowing the coachee to explore and understand their own.

- **Level Two** is passive. Here we tend to listen more carefully but are more concerned with content than feeling; we remain emotionally detached from the conversation. Useful for minute taking, essential if recording the content of a disciplinary interview, but not much use in a coaching conversation where it is just as important to demonstrate that we are listening as it is to listen in the first place.
- **Level Three** is active listening: hearing that picks up emotion, body language, and the context of what is being said.

Levels One and Two listen primarily for words. Level Three picks up everything else, including all of the sensory data as well as mood, pace and energy.

For many of us the ability to operate at Level Three has dulled over time, but the good news is that it can be honed again quite quickly. Try to practise Level Three listening in situations other than coaching and see what happens to the quality of exchange. Try encouraging speakers by using verbal and non-verbal prompts. Nodding, raising eyebrows, smiling, using 'I see', or 'Do go on' are all ways to help you concentrate on your listening and encourage the speaker to continue. Summaries and using the speaker's own words also serve to reinforce rapport and demonstrate that we are truly listening.

I sometimes think that coaching is like being a potter: you can do nothing without any clay. The clay in a coaching conversation is quality thinking and answers to questions, and it's your listening that will really draw it out.

Summary

This chapter has taught us that far from being a mystical method available only to the chosen few, coaching is a straightforward process available to any manager willing to invest a little time and effort in getting the best from their people, time and effort which will be repaid many times over.

Good coaches ask questions. If I'm to answer your coaching questions I'm going to need to think, to observe what goes on around me and to become more sensitised to those things. I'm also going to have to think beyond the obvious, to consider more imaginative solutions and to recognise the involvement I can have in my work. If all I'm ever asked to do is follow your instructions, my thinking muscles will atrophy, I will become reliant on you to tell me what I need to do and how I need to do it or I will become so frustrated at not really being able to participate in my work that I will essentially give up and do the minimum necessary to keep out of trouble.

Good coaches observe. How I am sends more signals about my levels of confidence and motivation than what I say. Good coaches (and good managers) have always known this and are careful to observe their team members, certainly within coaching conversations but as part of day-to-day working together too. How are people sitting and moving around? What is the physical reaction to the latest good news or the announcement of yet another setback? This is all good feedback which can be used to ensure real quality in any formal coaching sessions.

Good coaches listen. More than anything else good coaches listen. I listen to my wife when she asks me to help her with a job around the house, but if I'm watching sport or reading the paper and respond with a simple 'yes dear', I'm just hearing and not really listening at all. I listen to my friends when I'm out socialising, but if my mind is busy rehearsing my next contribution or I'm constantly interrupting and finishing their sentences, I'm not listening anything like as well as I could. The people we coach deserve much, much better than this. They deserve to be listened to as if they are the most important person in the world. They deserve to be listened to as if they have the most vital piece of information we could ever hope top hear. They deserve to be listened to at this level because even if we do nothing else, things will improve.

We should also consider ways of allowing our coachees to voice other things they are thinking and feeling about the situation as this will signal that you are a trustworthy coach who is willing to listen beyond the superficial level. Asking 'What else?' also gives you an opportunity to think about how the coaching is progressing and the question you would like to ask next, as well as encouraging a deeper level of thought in the coachee.

INSTANT TIP

Within the questioning style, make liberal use of 'What else?'

05

What principles are involved?

Introduction

You could finish the book here if you wanted to. Armed with my example questions you could go off and find someone to coach, sit them down, pose the questions, observe their responses closely and listen sagely and earnestly as the answers flow. You could do all this, but you would not really be coaching. It's unlikely that reeling off the questions would do any harm and actually it might do quite a lot of good, but as I've been at pains to stress, there is so much more to coaching than this.

This chapter is devoted to supporting what you've already learnt by identifying the principles that underpin the structure I've described. As with any structure if the foundations are weak what we build on top will be weak and likely to fail under pressure.

We'll see how the coaching approach depends on us having an optimistic view of people's capabilities and potential. Often called the *positive philosophical choice*, this viewpoint acknowledges that if we are to expect people to believe in themselves, *we* must believe in them first. We'll also explore how often people get in their own way and how questioning and listening identifies and dispels these self-imposed limitations. We need also to revisit the subject of motivation to see how we can incorporate motivational ideas into the coaching approach.

I will show you how good coaching raises *awareness*, generates *responsibility* and builds *trust*. For me these are the three cornerstones – if you can have three corners! – of all effective coaching.

Raising awareness brings people back to the here and now, to a point where they can make changes. Before we can improve anything we need to increase our awareness of how it is now. When we do this, improvement is often automatic. We'll see how coaching looks at people at work as responsible, i.e. with the capabilities they need to do what needs to be done – quite literally 'response-able'. We want the people we coach to leave a session with a plan of what they're going to do, not having transferred all their problems to us. I'll illustrate how coaching works best in an environment of trust and how the absence of such a climate can defeat even the slickest questioning, listening and observing.

All of these principles combine to bring about a state of mind in the coachee that we might call focused. I have found that focus is the quality that most distinguishes the outstanding performer from the average and so this is where our detailed examination of coaching principles will start.

Focus

The ability to achieve a state of focus is surely the greatest asset any employee could have in today's chaotic world of work. When someone is focused they work with a quiet concentration that seems almost eerie. When someone is focused they achieve results with half the effort of their huffing and puffing colleagues and become so conscious of what's going on that every task becomes a learning experience. Athletes talk of being 'in the zone', actors talk of being 'in flow', but these are all just alternative expressions of being focused. For many people it is a state they have experienced only rarely and often fleetingly when they do. However, it is a state that can be cultivated and I aim to show how the coaching approach achieves just that, but first we need to ensure we're clear about exactly what focus is.

Focus distracts us from being distracted. When we're focused we're almost oblivious to other things that are going on around us as anyone who has experienced the condition will readily testify. Watch a teenager absorbed in a new computer game and you'll see exactly what effective focus is like.

Focus follows interest though, which means that before we can expect anyone to focus on their work or critical aspects of certain tasks we must take time to ensure that they'll be interested. Many will be, but with other team members we may need to create interest firstly by explaining the requirements of a given task, emphasising its importance and underlining any key connections with other work activity.

Focus needs to be appropriate, which in a work context normally means focusing on what is to be achieved rather than what is to be avoided. At the Aims stage it's therefore important to set goals in positive language: 'Achieving quality standards' is better than 'Minimise wastage'; 'Keep spending within budget' is better than 'No overspends'.

Ideally we should allow people to focus on one thing at a time. However, this is virtually impossible in any modern place of work and so we need to try to minimize the numerous different areas of focus that vie for most people's attention. A member of your team may well have ten things to do, but they do them better in sequence rather than in parallel. This may mean some changes in the way that the work of your team is organised and distributed but it will be well worth the effort.

Imagine you work in a customer relations type role and I say to you, 'What do you most notice about the tone of your customer's voice?' To answer my question you'll need to focus on the customer's voice, which is of course exactly what I want you to do! But asking you about customer tone rather than instructing you to concentrate upon it raises your *awareness*, encourages you to take *responsibility* and demonstrates that I *trust* you. Thus focus combines these three key coaching principles.

Trust

I believe that increasing and improving levels of trust in organisations would make a massive difference. The absence of trust leads to a host of unnecessary, time-consuming, and bureaucratic processes that few people would miss if they disappeared. If we can't trust people not to fiddle their expenses do we really want them let loose on our customers and suppliers where they could do far more damage? Rather than tying managers up in 'back to work' interviews would it not be better to have them examine a culture so deficient that people would rather lie about their health than come in to work? Call me naive but I believe that there is a better way and that a coaching approach facilitates it. Let's first examine the components of trust in a coaching relationship. These are set out in the letter, opposite.

To be a manager who coaches thus requires a high level of integrity and trustworthiness and quite right too. Managers who coach in a climate of trust find they have advantages when things go wrong and/or pressure builds because their people are more willing to 'go into bat' for them when needs be. People who work for managers they cannot trust or who don't believe they are trusted themselves tend not to do this, and in extreme cases they will look to sabotage the manager's efforts

Dear Manager

I need to trust you, my coaching manager. This requires you to be a trustworthy person doing trustworthy things. I need to know that anything I might reveal in a coaching session will be treated in confidence unless I am up to something illegal, unethical or harmful. I need to know that discussing areas of my work that I find challenging will not automatically disbar me from applying for a promotion or some other advancement. I want to be able to turn to you for coaching help, whether to solve a problem or make progress on an already strong area. I want you to make time for me and our coaching conversations, to be taken seriously and for you to accept I have a point of view, even if it differs from your own.

I need to trust the coaching process. I don't want to be coached if I neither need it nor have requested it. I don't want to be coached just because it's my turn or because you've got a schedule to stick to. Do it this way if you want (and far too many do) but don't be surprised if I don't seem fully engaged. Don't be surprised if I offer only superficial answers to your coaching questions and seem mistrustful of the whole thing. It'll be because I sense it is all about you and not me.

Help me to trust myself. To become the best I can be and achieve my potential at work I need someone who believes in me, even when I've lost faith in myself. You're my manager; I respect your position and what you've achieved and your backing and support means a lot. With it I can achieve great things which creates a 'win' for you, me and our organisation alike. Without it we all lose in the end.

Thank you.

Responsibility

I once worked in an office where I sat near to the senior manager's secretary/PA. This awful woman fulfilled every negative stereotype associated with such a role – she was difficult and truculent and made most people's lives a misery. On top of this she could be aptly described as work shy and idle...

...except for two weeks in every year.

These were the two weeks when her boss, the senior manager, was on holiday. During this period she would be responsible for managing his diary commitments, handling requests from other senior members of staff, signing purchase orders and a host of other tasks that were very, very different from her normal job. At these times she was a pleasure to work alongside and got through a staggering amount of work.

What could explain the difference? It wasn't just relief that her boss was away, because he was a genuinely nice and capable person for whom we all enjoyed working. It wasn't because the tasks she now undertook were glamorous and fulfilling because they weren't. It was because she was responsible and knew it. If a conflicting diary appointment occurred when the boss was there, she made him aware of it and *he* decided what to do. If someone wanted to raise a purchase order when he was in, *he* decided if the money could be paid away. In his absence, she made these decisions – she was responsible and she had *choice*. There was a chance she could have made mistakes but I cannot recall a time when she did.

This is the magic of responsibility. How many times have you seen the wayward sports team member be transformed by being given the captaincy? The sports manager understands the power of responsibility and giving people choice in order to make them feel empowered. It can turn the poacher into the gamekeeper overnight. The next time you're thinking about how cynical old Brian from accounts may react to the latest changes to the office procedures, think about what might change if Brian were to be invited to take responsibility for changing the office procedures. Notice I say invited, because responsibility must be taken up – it must be accepted, it cannot be imposed.

Coaching is about getting the best 'out' of people, which implies that it's there to begin with, but people will only choose to give of their very best if they feel capable of doing so, when they're rewarded for doing so and when they're willing to try. You can use coaching to make sure these three elements are in place or to uncover any blockages.

The coaching questions in the ARROW model (see Chapter 4) are designed to generate responsibility, e.g. 'What are YOU going to do?', 'When are YOU going to do it?' etc. It's OK for you to put people on the spot a little bit with these sorts of questions, and we need to if we really want to improve performance at work. While we continue to do things for people that they can (and sometimes need) to do for themselves we actually have not helped at all.

Awareness

- How comfortable would you like to feel as you sit reading this book?
- How comfortable are you feeling right now?
- How much difference is there between the two?
- What could you change to get more comfortable?
- What are you going to do?

A quick coaching session using the ARROW sequence (did you spot it?) on increasing comfort. All founded on making you more *aware* of the state of comfort. Aware of the state of comfort that you have, aware of the state of comfort that you want and aware of what you can alter to get more comfortable. Coaching is all about change and improvement, but before we can change or improve anything we must increase our awareness of how it is now.

Try this. Think of an item you know well but that you can't actually see. For example, if you're sitting reading this in your living room, think about, say, your alarm clock in the bedroom. If you're reading this on the train on your way to work, think of, say, the contents of the top drawer in your desk. Grab a paper and pen and draw whatever item you're thinking of in as much detail as you can. Think of every feature, think of the colour, the shape, the texture and size and try to capture these things as accurately as you can. Now go and find the item in question and compare it with your drawing. You've probably missed some important details or got some features wrong. You may even have included some aspects that aren't actually there at all. At a seminar I ran recently, I asked all the attendees to give me their watch at the start. Twenty minutes into the talk, I asked them to draw their watches in a similar way to I've asked you here. One guy was stunned. He'd carefully shown beautiful Roman numerals on his drawing only to discover there were none on his watch when I returned it. 'I can't believe I did that' he mumbled for the rest of the talk.

What this shows is how little use we make of our awareness in everyday working life. We move through the working day in a sort of daydream; we think we're aware of what's happening but in truth we are not. Think what might happen with our awareness increased. The things we'd see, the details we'd notice. We'd read other people's reactions better and become much more sensitive as a result. We'd understand our own feelings better, be less susceptible to them and more able to take control. We'd notice the subtle differences in the tone of voice of our customers and colleagues as they respond to the content and style of our own communication. Things would improve just by a process of taking better notice. That's all we'd have to do – it would be that easy. Coaching brings about this state of increased awareness.

Performance, learning and enjoyment (PLE)

I want to return now to the subject of motivation, but this time to consider how a knowledge of motivation can become a guiding principle for effective coaches. In Chapter 4 we considered a range of both *external* and *internal* motivators and the various theories that can help us provide a climate in which motivation can flourish. We know that the internal group tends to motivate over the longer term but that organisations spend more time fretting over the external set. This irony is extended when we consider how much more costly the external set are to provide. As coaches we have much more power to work with the internal set, as these are felt or experienced by the employee whereas the external set are provided by the organisation and probably beyond our sphere of control.

There are internal motivators like pride, satisfaction, accomplishment, sense of achievement and so on which I like to group together as being matters of *performance*. There are then internal motivators such as curiosity, acquiring new skills, moving outside of comfort zones and trying new things. These we can group as being matters of *learning*. Finally we can consider internal motivators such as fun, finding work pleasant and enjoying the company of our colleagues as being matters of *enjoyment*. Thus the wide variety of internal motivators can be made easier to work with by being summarised as performance, learning and enjoyment (PLE) and I like to show them arranged on a triangle (see Figure 5.1).

The real trick here is to use coaching to keep a healthy balance of the three. Any one of the three which is over-stressed at the expense of the others leads to demotivation. Most people experience this when performance becomes all consuming. They have targets and standards and key performance indicators fired at them constantly and any sense of learning and enjoyment disappears. Doing a good job and hitting targets – performing – is highly motivating, but not without learning and enjoyment as well.

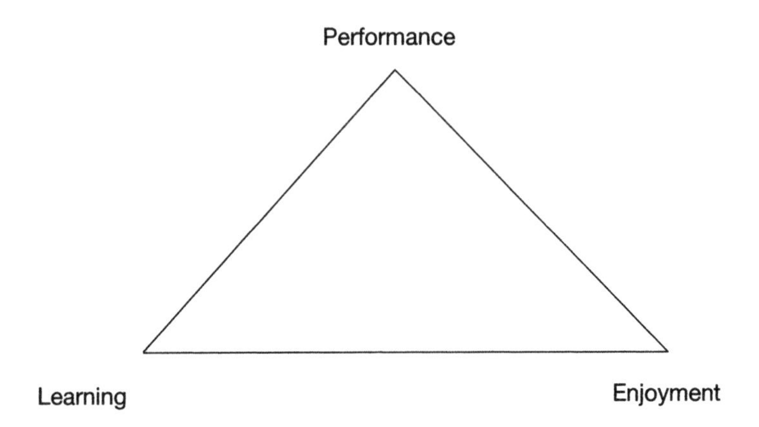

Figure 5.1: Internal motivators

I see this as all too common and have a theory that people join organisations on the expectation of PLE in balance and leave because learning and enjoyment disappears.

It is also possible to create an overbalance by having too much learning. Becoming more skilled, learning new technology and trying new things is great, but not if we never get a chance to put what we learn into practice or if the working atmosphere is so sour that we're still just a miserable as before. Believe it or not you can also upset internal motivation by having too much enjoyment. Of course it's great to work in a nice, fun atmosphere, but not if we're given meaningless tasks and nothing ever changes.

I've said all along that coaching is about performance improvement, but what makes it so much more effective than other development approaches is that it is hugely insightful for the person being coached and – when done well – is a highly enjoyable process. Coaching hits the dead centre of the PLE triangle

Interference

Stop! I know this chapter is about espousing the principles of successful coaching, but I am NOT about to recommend that coaches interfere with the learning and performance of their coachees. Quite the reverse in fact. Good coaches appreciate the value of *responsibility* and are strong enough to *trust* the coachee to figure things out themselves with their support rather than their interference. What part then can interference possibly play in the coaching domain?

The successful performance of any task at work depends as much on the degree to which we interfere with our abilities – getting in our own way – as it does on those abilities themselves. Tim Gallwey – for many people the founder of modern coaching – expressed this deceptively simple idea as a formula:

$$P = p - i$$

In this equation P stands for performance, in other words the results your efforts achieve. Similarly, p refers to potential, defined as your innate ability – what you might actually be capable of given the right conditions. Finally, i means interference – the things that meddle with that potential being converted into results.

Conventional training and development approaches try to improve performance (P) by improving potential. That means imbuing the performer with new knowledge and skills and providing encouragement and opportunities to use them. If we take a coaching approach and seek to reduce interference (i) at the same time as potential (p) is being trained then we can help people operate at a level of performance much closer to their true potential. I believe most people know this intuitively when they say 'we must use coaching to get the best out of people'. This statement implies that the best is already inside people and what we have to do is remove the impediments (interference) to its expression.

We can once again categorise interference as being either external or internal. Typical examples of external interference include:

- policies
- procedures
- boss's style
- organisation culture

These are all very subjective of course, but if the employee feels these things are getting in the way, then they probably are. For most coaching managers though there may be little to be done with these other than acknowledge their existence and sympathise with any frustration caused.

However, we can have a much more profound effect by helping people identify and deal with sources of internal interference, for example:

- self-doubt
- limiting beliefs
- negative memories
- unhelpful self-talk

Coaching at work recognises the discomfort these interferences can cause even though we may not even be aware of them at a conscious level. However, as with coaching for sport, discomfort is a sign of inefficiency and so we must acknowledge the discomfort first before we can move on.

Coaching does not deny the existence of these interferences or suggest that they are easily removed by incanting affirmations or practising bizarre visualisation exercises. We've seen already that coaching creates focus and focus is the most powerful antidote to interference. The more focused I become of the aspects of my work situation that are conducive to success, the less I'm aware of the nagging doubts, inappropriate procedures or whatever else is getting in my way.

Potential

- Do the people in your team have the potential to perform at the level you need them to or that they would like to?
- Can you prove it?

Whatever your answer to the first question, I'll bet you answered 'no' to the second.

Human potential (and indeed human nature) cannot be proven and so we are left to take a view. In other words, we must choose a philosophy of human potential. Some managers (like Gene whom we met in the Preface) take a rather negative view of people's potential and suggest that it is deployed at work only in response to threat or reward and then only to a degree necessary to keep out of trouble. Others take a less jaundiced view (such as Sam) and opt to see potential as limitless given appropriate support and guidance. I don't know which view is right or wrong and I have no interest in finding out. I do however know which view offers the most possibilities and so I choose to make the positive philosophical choice and would encourage you to do likewise. I hope the book so far has taken your thinking to a point where this is easy for you to do.

In so far as high-quality thinking and self-prompted action is encouraged when negative, limiting assumptions are removed in the process of coaching, a positive view of potential has to be present before anything else can happen. This philosophy has proven time and again to be the best one from which to free the mind to think clearly, creatively and in the best interests of self, team and organisation. Ideas and actions flow more dependably from this philosophy than from a more neutral or cynical one.

Most people at work function at levels well below that of their potential. At the leaving celebration for the manager's PA I wrote about earlier in this chapter (see the section on Responsibility), we found out that she worked as a volunteer for the Samaritans (a charitable support organisation offering phone support to depressed and lonely people). This was hard to reconcile to the old grump we saw every day at work, but the potential to be a warm and considerate person was clearly always there, it just wasn't being cultivated in the work situation. Many people are just not given an opportunity to reach into their potential and in the face of such interference become accustomed to just doing enough.

Sometimes a crisis draws potential out. A manufacturing business I worked with claimed that their people were already doing all they could to get the product out of the door as fast as they could. They would love to achieve more and process orders faster, but there was just no capacity left. One day a major customer of theirs threatened to take his business elsewhere unless an order could be fulfilled by the end of that week. The entire staff got together and found new ways to speed up production and strip out needless processes. The order was fulfilled and the day was saved. The potential to perform at this level was always there, it just needed a crisis to bring it out. Coaching helps us tap into this potential without turning every working day into an emergency.

Summary

This chapter has been devoted to setting out the principles which provide the foundation for the skill-based work of questioning, listening and observing. These principles have not been shown as models or formulas, but each has been explored as a stand alone principle in its own right. Given the scope of this work it might be sensible to consider making any of these principles the subject of your special attention as time passes. You may, for example, feel that an upcoming project requires the best *focus* you can help your team muster. On other occasions you may feel as if you're personally taking too much on and would prefer to spread some *responsibility*. However, this summary provides an opportunity to show how the principles are linked.

We start with considering whether the people we coach have the potential to perform. Our work here is subject to the phenomenon of the self-fulfilling prophecy. The view we have of people's potential (and abilities) will influence how we behave towards them and they will respond in kind. It seems right therefore to adopt an optimistic philosophy.

The job of people management is to turn potential into performance, whether that be sales generated, costs contained or any of the myriad business outcomes we're trying to achieve. Between potential and performance there is interference. There is external interference which can sometimes be altered or eliminated and there is internal interference. The effects of self-doubt and negative expectations are not so easily vanquished but the effects can be dimmed by finding a better point of focus.

With interference under control more potential is converted into performance and a higher level of performance is a potent internal motivator. When this is combined and balanced with learning and enjoyment the chances of achieving sustainable high performance increase exponentially.

The combination of inquisitive questioning, careful listening and alert observation employed by coaches in their communication style, throws light on what might be causing interference and where performance, learning and enjoyment may be out of balance. This is because we are raising awareness, generating responsibility and building trust and these are always components of sustainable high performance in any sphere. The coaching conversation I have with you helps me to become aware of interference and imbalance, encourages me to take responsibility for making changes and helps me to trust you and myself to move forward from that point.

All of this work goes on in the mind of course, for it is at the level of my thinking that I must make changes first. Your coaching helps me achieve a mental state of being aware, responsible and trusting and this state can best be labelled focused.

INSTANT TIP

Always remember that coaching is an a.r.t (awareness, responsibility, trust). Developing these facets in the people whom you coach will always pay dividends.

06

What attributes do I need?

Introduction

Have a look at the extract from a recent job advertisement set out on the following page.

This is not a specific coaching job, but a general management position. Nevertheless, coaching is mentioned twice and the other italicized words are both required of the effective coach and a product of their effective coaching. This advert is typical for management positions and these requirements are likely to become more prevalent as the need to be effective as the people side of the management role becomes more crucial.

The job is for a Branch Manager at a retail bank, yet there is no mention of needing previous banking experience or to hold that profession's qualifications. The essential elements of the job are those on the people management side.

It seems then that, as well as considering coaching methods and principles as we have done in the last two chapters, we must also consider the attributes or personal qualities required as the roles of coach and manager are synonymous in these current times.

Do you want to join one of the UK's leading companies with rewards and benefits to match? This is an excellent opportunity to work for an extremely successful financial organization which is also renowned for its excellent salary schemes. They also offer work flexibility and a training and development programme with fast-moving career progression opportunities for the right candidate.

As the Branch Manager you will be responsible for *achieving* and *exceeding* service, sales and control *targets* by *managing*, *coaching* and *motivating* the Branch team to *deliver outstanding customer service*. You also ensure the branch team *delivers* results whilst following the Bank's service and sales processes and procedures.

The role will also involve coaching and *training to build professionalism and knowledge*. You will also be responsible for inducting new staff and *supporting their development*, and managing the resourcing of the branch to make sure it is working to maximum capacity to provide excellent customer service. This will be achieved through regular meetings with the team to *encourage and motivate* them, thus ensuring that sales opportunities and customer service are optimised.

Sales team management experience is essential, preferably within retail banking although strong career-minded managers from a retail background may also be considered.

The successful candidate must have experience in *leading*, *motivating* and *influencing* a banking sales team. You will also be passionate about providing a world-class level of service and have the ability to lead from the front.

In return you will be rewarded with a competitive salary and excellent benefits package tailored to your individual requirements.

We will not concern ourselves with the semantic differences between knowledge, skills and attributes but consider the main qualities of the effective coaching manager. There is a great list I could have chosen from, but I have decided to go with the ones that come in answer when I pose the question: 'On what basis would you choose your own coach?'

Expertise

One area in which there seems to be a difference of opinion amongst coaching commentators is the degree to which coaches need background expertise in the issue under discussion. John Whitmore challenges whether a coach needs to have *any* experience or technical knowledge in the area in which he or she is coaching. He goes on to state that such experience and expertise is not necessary, providing the coach is truly acting as the detached awareness raiser with an absolute belief in the potential of the coachee and the value of self-responsibility. My own experience bears this out and I have personally coached managers in areas such as process reengineering and information technology – areas in which I have no expertise whatsoever. In this situation the key as ever is to ask good coaching questions and to listen carefully in order to help these managers set sensible goals and to assist them in finding the resources required to meet those goals.

Others take a different view. Freelance consultant and facilitator Trevor Bentley, for example, states emphatically that the coach must be able to 'model' what he or she requires the coachee to do:

> *The whole coaching approach is for someone who is trusted, with knowledge and experience to help someone less experienced but with skills and talent, to develop.*
>
> Trevor Bentley, 'Performance Coaching',
> (*Training Officer*, 1995)

For me this seems more like a mentoring approach and difficult to sustain in such changing times. I also think it could provide an opportunity for the less than scrupulous coaching manager to disguise telling as coaching.

For many, the issue of expertise in coaching is resolved by classifying the coaching as directive or non-directive.

The non-directive school suggests that coaches help the coachee explore a situation, identify some options and select a way forward. It is the coachee that takes full ownership of the solution and the actions required. Directive coaching relies on instruction and guidance from the coach and is thus limited by their knowledge. Even proponents of the directive approach acknowledge that the responsibility for the solution is seldom successfully transferred to the coachee.

My view is that any notion of directive coaching moves too far towards instruction and teaching type interventions which are to be avoided if coaching is really to bring about a change in management approach. The effective coach does not need to have expertise in the area being coached. Rather they will use effective questioning skills to help the coachee develop their own, unique insight. Put more crudely, the effective coach takes the positive stance that 'the brain that has the problem is the brain with the solution'.

So, you need expertise to *teach*, but not to coach. A background in the issue at hand may be useful for establishing credibility but it is not essential. In fact, it may increase the temptation to tell and as such it is often easier to coach without the baggage of expertise.

Ability to provide constructive feedback

Let me say firstly that I am extremely dubious about the quality and value of the typical feedback offered at work. It is usually thinly veiled criticism or destructive, judgemental nonsense that does neither giver nor receiver any good. It creates new sources of interference and results in awareness and focus collapsing rather than being enhanced.

However, giving the people you coach solid, *constructive* feedback *can* be an extremely valuable part of effective coaching, but only if it is done well. This means that the feedback needs to be free of value judgements and offered as pure information. This is easier said than done. Bear in mind as well that you can only give feedback on what you see or hear. You cannot give feedback on how the person felt – this is their domain – but it might be precisely where the problem lies. Finally, remember that the best feedback is self-realised and this is best achieved through questioning. Nevertheless, there will be times when you'll want to offer feedback and the following hints and tips will help.

- **Start with the positive.** People need encouragement and to be told when they are doing well – it will help the receiver to hear first what you have observed them doing well. If the positive is registered first the negative is more likely to be listened to. This approach also helps to balance out our natural tendency to dwell on any perceived negative points.
- **Be specific.** Avoid general comments like 'you are really great' or 'that was not so good'. These types of comments do not give enough detail to be useful sources of development. Pinpoint if possible exactly what was 'good', etc.
- **Question whether behaviour change is possible.** Don't give people feedback about something over which they have no control, e.g. 'you'd be more assertive if you were taller'. Instead give people something to work on, e.g. 'the customer responded with more enthusiasm when you spoke slightly faster'.

- **Offer alternatives.** If you do give negative feedback then don't simply criticise but suggest what the person could have done differently. This can turn the negative feedback into a positive way forward.
- **Be descriptive not evaluative.** Tell the person what you saw and heard and the effect it had on you rather than merely saying something was 'good' or 'bad', e.g. 'your tone of voice as you said that made me feel you were really concerned'.
- **Own it.** If you say 'You are...' it gives the impression that you are offering a universally agreed opinion on that person. You should only give your opinion of people at that particular time. Similarly, begin you feedback with 'I...' or 'In my opinion...'. If a third party has brought something to your attention try to corroborate the facts first and make it your own feedback when it's offered.

There is a difference between negative feedback and feedback on a negative situation or outcome. Remember that in itself, feedback is neither positive nor negative – it is simply information.

Self-awareness

In the last chapter we examined the principle of awareness and saw that before anything can improve we must first increase our awareness of how it is now. This applies to us as coaching managers as much as anything else. We too must increase awareness of how we are – how we are coaching now and the effects of our own behaviour – alongside raising awareness of these things in those whom we coach to move forward.

The Johari window (see Figure 6.1) is a very useful model for developing self-awareness. It was conceived by Joe Luft and Harry Ingram (hence the name) as a means of identifying interpersonal communication style. It suggests there are two sources from which we learn about our impact and communication style: ourselves and others.

	known to self	not known to self
known to others	open	blind
known to others	secret	unknown

Figure 6.1: The Johari window

- **The open area** includes behaviour, thoughts and feelings that both we and others know. The fact that we and others hold similar information creates more effective personal communication. In fact, the underlying assumption of the whole model is that the effectiveness of our personal communication increases the larger this window becomes.
- **The blind area** represents aspects not known to ourselves but readily apparent to others. The red-faced, scowling manager shouting, 'I'm not angry!' and the customer saying, 'Yes, I understand' whilst frowning and looking puzzled are classic examples.
- **The secret area** represents the thoughts and feelings we keep to ourselves. The secret area represents a large part of our behaviour when amongst strangers – where not a lot is known about each other and trust is low.

- **The unknown area** represents the most deeply rooted aspects of our personality which are not apparent to ourselves or others around us. It is really the realm of highly trained psychologists and of less importance in everyday coaching although we may conclude that our untapped potential lies in this area.

If we agree that larger open windows lead to greater self-awareness and more effective communication, then the question becomes how do we enlarge the open window?

To widen the open window – that is to have fewer 'secrets'; and fewer things 'not known to others' – requires us to disclose. As managers who coach we need to be prepared to take a lead on this and be willing to share things with our coachee that may initially feel uncomfortable. This can include revealing that you are new to coaching and anxious about 'getting it right' or 'doing it well'. This can also act as a powerful way of building trust and demonstrating the value of not holding things back.

To deepen the open window – that is to have fewer 'blind spots' and fewer things 'not known to ourselves' – requires effective feedback. This means as coaches we need to be open to feedback and encourage our coachees to tell us what they valued about our coaching, what they would have liked more of or less of, etc.

Effective listening skills

I know we've already considered listening in Chapter 3 when we explored how we actually coach, but it is such a vital component of effective coaching and such a key skill for the effective coach that I want to offer some more guidance here. We spend roughly 70 per cent of our waking hours in some form of verbal communication but few of us have ever had any formal training in the art of listening. We need to be open to any suggestions that might help us improve. So here goes.

- **Never rule out any topic of discussion as uninteresting.** As a coach always be on the lookout for new information. While the content of the conversation may be dull (to you) there is always something to be learned, especially about the art of communication.
- **Accept the coachee's reality.** This is not an exhortation to believe almost anything anyone tells you. The point is to suspend judgement during the immediate experience of listening. In initially accepting what the coachee says, you're not confirming things as 'true', you're simply acknowledging exactly what the speaker is saying – right or wrong, good or bad, true or false. This capacity for total acceptance frees the mind to listen for other clues.
- **Listen for the whole message.** One estimate has it that 75 per cent of all communication is non-verbal. Beyond the words themselves is a host of clues as to what the speaker is communicating. What do you notice about the posture the coachee has adopted? Is it rigid or relaxed, 'closed' or 'open'? When the coachee answers your coaching questions what can you tell from their facial expression? Specifically, does it support the words? What about their hands? Are they clenched, open, relaxed, tense? Does the coachee maintain eye contact? Does the tone of voice match the words? What do you notice about the coachee's movements? Are they intense or relaxed, congruent – in keeping with the content of what's being said – or conflicting? Does the way they are communicating seem 'staged'? What you're looking for here are inconsistencies between what is said and what is really meant, clues that tell you the spoken message isn't really genuine.
- **Don't get hung up on the coachee's delivery style.** Above and beyond what was outlined above, there are also factors that simply reveal unease in delivery rather than any attempt to mislead. The key is being able to

distinguish between the two. It's easy to get turned off when someone speaks haltingly, has an irritating voice, or just doesn't come across well. The key to good listening, however, is to get beyond the manner of delivery to the underlying message. In order for this to happen, you have to resolve not to judge the message by the delivery style. It's amazing how much more clearly you can 'hear' once you've made the decision to really listen rather than to criticise.

- **Avoid structured listening.** Structured listening refers to the idea of adopting a format for listening, either in the form of posing mental questions, e.g. 'What is the coachee's main point?', 'What are they *really* saying?', or by monitoring for key words, e.g. problem, solution, future, past. The problem with this approach is that it creates a dialogue in the listener's mind which we can recognise as internal interference. I think it's better to keep an open mind and receive the information just as it comes, without any attempt to structure or judge it.
- **Tune out distractions.** Replace them with a focus on the speaker. Poor listeners are distracted by interruptions; good listeners tune them out and focus on the speaker and the message. This is easier said than done of course and we know from looking at focus earlier on that even when it's achieved it's easily lost. Try to maintain eye contact with the coachee; lean forward in your chair; let their words settle in your ears; and turn in your chair, if necessary, to block out unwanted distractions. Put your PDA and mobile in a drawer, pull the blinds, do whatever you need to do to focus on your coachee.
- **Be alert to your own prejudices.** We all have them and we need to think specifically about the impact of our prejudices on our ability to really hear what's being communicated. Often, we are unaware how strongly our prejudices influence our willingness and ability to hear.

The fact is: any prejudice, valid or not, tends to obscure the message.

- **Resist the temptation to argue.** Why is it that, when we hear someone saying something with which we strongly disagree, we immediately begin mentally formulating a counter argument? There are many reasons of course, but one of the most common is our natural tendency to resist any new information that conflicts with what we believe. Bear in mind that you can always put forward an argument later, when you've heard the whole message and had time to think about it.
- **Take notes but only if it helps.** There's a scale of opinion when it comes to the place of note-taking in effective coaching. At one end, is the argument that coaching is about thinking and note-taking simply creates interference. Others contend that copious notes and detailed action plans are an absolute necessity. I'm personally ambivalent about note-taking. If you can listen and take notes at the same time, great. If you can't, do without note-taking or record key words only (or even key images/doodles) or pause every now and then for summary notes. Experiment and find what suits you best. One strong feeling I do have is that we should not ask the coachee to take notes *during* the session – they should be free to think – but that it's fine to ask them to record a summary afterwards.

Empathy

Let's remember that our coachees will be doing a lot of listening too. They will likewise be noticing what we say and how we say it, and monitoring our body language in much the same way as we'll monitor theirs. I would contend that what the coachee *hears* is more important than what the coach *says* and there is often a big difference between the two. Once again, working with the coachee's reality will lead to a greater level of trust and a more insightful conversation for both parties. To do so requires us to use empathy. Within the context of coaching, empathy refers to better anticipating how the coachee will respond to a message or to an invitation to think in answer to a coaching question. This ability to appreciate the thoughts, feelings and intentions of another person is sometimes known as transposing or more colloquially as 'walking a mile in another person's shoes'.

We can see how this would be particularly useful in thinking through how we might introduce coaching or in preparing to coach an individual for the first time. Put yourself in the position of a person being coached for the first time and ask yourself, 'What am I thinking?', 'What am I feeling?', 'What do I want?' Given the misinformation that abounds regarding coaching and the unhelpful associations it has with things like counselling and psychotherapy we might assume that the coachee is thinking: 'What have I done wrong? Why me? What am I poor at? Is everyone getting this or am I being singled out?' The coachee is possibly feeling anxious, defensive, guarded and wary. In light of these thoughts and feelings he or she will want to get through the session or conversation as quickly as possible and with their dignity intact. We could accurately label all of this mental activity as interference and it would take a miraculous bit of coaching to get past it all and find a more useful and appropriate focus.

Fortunately, in reality reactions to the prospect of being coached vary a lot. Other people will approach coaching with positive feelings of excitement and curiosity. The point is we can see the value of appreciating things from another's standpoint and how important it is to acknowledge the thoughts and feelings of the coachee. We must take the time to position coaching properly before we can expect it to do any good. Above all, we need to keep an open mind.

I also like the idea that 'empathy is sympathy in action' which means that when someone describes a problem it is much more useful for us to ask, 'What do you intend to do and when do you intend to do it?' than just say 'Oh, isn't that awful for you!'

Other important attributes

Before we go on, a moment's reflection. We've considered the place of expertise in the make-up of the effective coach and hopefully you're now convinced that expertise in coaching is more important than expertise in the matter at hand. We've also looked at feedback, self-awareness, listening and empathy. These attributes alone will serve you extremely well as a coaching manager but there are other attributes, albeit less crucial ones, that need briefly to be considered too.

Credibility

You don't need to be an expert, but you do need to be credible. You need to be a good role model for the behaviours you're encouraging others to develop and you need to know enough about what's going on to at least be able to know the right questions to ask. You're likely to be manager and coach to the same group of people and so your credibility is probably established anyway. Just be wary of this turning into being seen as the one who must have all the answers.

Trust

Trust is one of the key principles of coaching and one component of trust is encouraging the people whom we coach to trust themselves. If you watch small children play and try new things you'll know that they trust themselves instinctively. It must be as adults that doubts, fear, limiting beliefs and so on accumulate over time. The job of the coach is to help our people *unlearn* such things. This then also requires trust in the coach and trust in the coaching process.

Dislike of mediocrity

As a coaching manager, we are going to want very high standards. Good enough must no longer be good enough. Whilst we understand the dangers of setting the bar too high when goal setting and so on, we must also recognise the need to encourage people to really go for it when seeking to convert potential into performance. In a similar way I have noticed that organisations with a coaching culture seem to set their standards in absolute rather than relative terms. In other words they are concerned less about beating the competition and more about being the best they can be.

Patience

Coaching on a relatively straightforward, task-related situation will produce results immediately. Coaching on more complex subjects requires a degree of patience as high-quality thinking can take a little time to find momentum, and because people think and act at different speeds. The rewards are there but the manager who coaches may also need to act as a buffer to the pressure and short-termism that may create a cacophony of interference in the minds of the team and so prevent real learning and progress. Of course you're not immune from these same pressures, so a little coaching from your boss or from a colleague may be required.

Detachment

The effective coaching manager is detached from the problems of the person being coached. As a coach and a manager this is a much harder trick to pull off than for the independent coach. However, you are much more use to your coachees if you can remain objective and allow them to explore their own ways forward – you're trying to generate responsibility after all. If you think this will be a problem for you, write 'How detached am I?' on a sticky note and place it where you'll see it from time to time.

Non-judgemental

Judgement is weedkiller to the flowers of awareness, responsibility and trust. Imagine that during the course of a coaching session I reveal that I find the Operations Director intimidating, that I think his behaviour is arrogant and that basically I'm scared of the guy. Imagine that your reaction is a perfectly innocuous, 'Oh, come on, you're being daft!' Let's see what that does. Firstly my awareness and focus has shifted to considering whether it's fair and just for you to say that, and if I think it isn't my focus now is on arguing my position. Next I'm thinking that this is not a problem I'm able to solve myself and that there's no point trying. Finally I'll be disappointed that despite trusting you with my revelation you've used it to have a little dig. I'll be less inclined to disclose things again.

Curiosity

Following this line of thinking, how then should you respond to my revelation? Asking questions would be a good start. When did that last happen? What exactly was said? How did you respond? How do you feel looking back? What could you have done differently? What different outcome may have come about? When do you next expect to have dealings with this person? How do you plan to handle it? Ask me these things and I have to direct my awareness and focus on the nuances of the problem, and as we now know awareness is half the battle or at least the first step. I'm also realising that I have choice and so I am responsible (able to respond). Finally I'm realising that you trust that I can learn how to deal with this and that you're not going to hold it against me. Curiosity and judgement are like two sides of the same coin, but in coaching they produce very different results.

Sense of humour and perspective

I used to work with a salesperson who, every time a sale was lost, would cry, 'Oh for heaven's sake nobody died!' An extreme reaction perhaps but one which does reveal a tendency to take ourselves too seriously and attach a bit too much importance to work. In fifty years, who's going to care?

Summary

How does all of this disparate information come together to give us a profile of an effective coaching manager? It would seem that the first requirement is for the manager to find time to coach, to take 'time out' from their own duties to provide regular coaching input. The coaching manager then establishes their credibility by undertaking their own job conscientiously and competently. They do not worry about being the fount of all wisdom for the entire team. A manager who coaches will endeavour to set a good example and be an appropriate role model, but they are secure enough to avoid 'pulling rank' or having to rely on position power, i.e. that which comes with the job description and place in the organisation's pecking order.

Managers who coach are natural advocates of their people, encouraging and supporting them, especially when things are not going well. They give praise when it is due, but deal with poor performance in a straightforward and understanding manner. Managers who coach treat each individual as a person in their own right – uniquely different from other employees with whom they interact at work.

So to be a coach in a work context, these are the attributes you must develop. But are these not the same attributes that we've always needed to be an effective manager of people at work? Whilst we use the terms 'coaches' and 'coaching', do we not simply mean employing the knowledge, skills and personal qualities that those people seen as effective people managers always have? Assuming you picked up this book because you are, or are about to become, a manager of people, I think you can afford to feel encouraged because you must already have these attributes developed to some degree anyway. You would not be in the job if you didn't. As managers of people we *are* coaches – and always have been – but we can certainly develop our capabilities and improve our results by becoming aware of the factors this chapter has highlighted.

INSTANT TIP

Make your own list of, say, the top ten coaching qualities (better still, ask your team to prepare the list). Award yourself marks out of ten for each of them. Use the coaching questions in Chapter 3 to self-coach on the ones that will make the greatest impact.

07

When should I use coaching?

Introduction

In my office we like to dine out on this little anecdote. A university lecturer we know phoned her HR department and asked 'How do I go about getting myself some coaching?' Their reply was, 'Why, what's wrong with you?' This mentality is something we must absolutely reject if we're to have any chance of coaching doing its job. Coaching is a fantastic tool to use in all manner of work situations – as we shall see – but only if it's positioned in a positive way.

So the question remains, when should you use coaching? I suppose the simple answer is, now! Get on with it! Look at all the benefits I've illustrated – why wait? But I realise you need a more refined answer than that. In this chapter I want to set out how coaching applies and works in a variety of typical *situations* at work. I'll do that by detailing some example coaching conversations. I hope that this will also illustrate how the coaching ARROW (see Chapter 4) and the principles that underpin it operate in everyday circumstances. But let's firstly consider what makes the average manager consider the coaching approach in the first place. After all, the typical work situations I'll examine are not new; they've been happening for decades, so why do we need a new approach to dealing with them? The answer lies in the ever decreasing effectiveness of the 'tell and instruct' approach.

Consider the following graph.

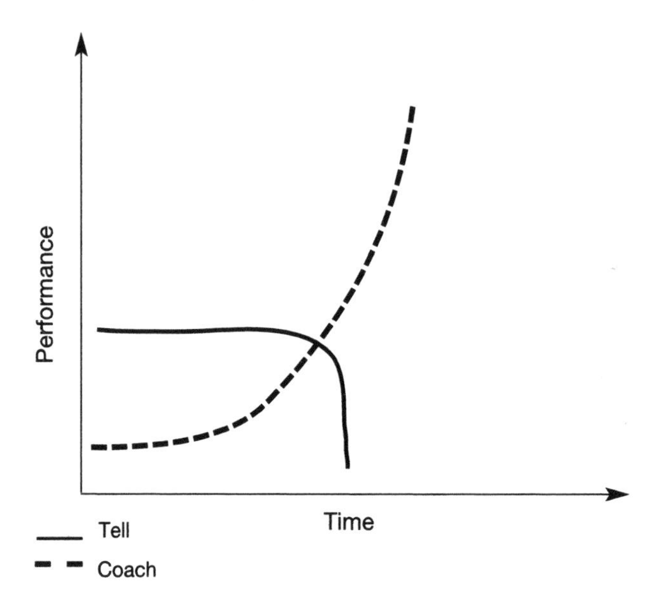

Figure 7.1: When coaching is effective

When somebody is new to the team, we obviously need to do a certain amount of telling. When people are new, they need information and instructions and it's arguably a little too soon to be asking for their views on the way forward (although you could really benefit from their objectivity). When time is short, or in crisis situations, we need also to tell people what to do, because the needs of the situation require it. There is no time for a debate and the risks of inaction outweigh the risks of doing the wrong thing. The tell style is perfectly appropriate in these situations, but when the crisis has passed and things have calmed down, telling becomes first inappropriate and eventually counterproductive. People have information and instructions but they now want to exercise a little responsibility.

Coaching is an investment of time and, like all longer term investments, the pay-off is not immediate. This can be unacceptable at work and even I would argue that it can sometimes be premature to coach or the timing can be wrong.

So the graph (Figure 7.1) illustrates a cross-over point where the effectiveness of telling falls dramatically and coaching comes into its own. Unfortunately there are no hard and fast rules for where this point lies for each individual whom you coach. The real trick is for you to become aware of their changing needs and circumstances and spot when it's time to switch lines.

Knowing when it's time to coach

Let's now consider the change in circumstances that would indicate a need to move from the more controlling 'tell what and how', to the more empowering (responsibility generating) coaching approach.

When learning from the experience is paramount, it's time to coach. There is very little learning that happens from the tell style apart from perhaps learning how to keep our heads down and learning how to cover up errors. Being told what to do does not engage our brains and so we do not forge new connections and insights; we do not learn. There is also the problem of recall, with one study showing that after three months participants could remember only 10 per cent of what they'd been told. Coaching, with its emphasis on awareness, responsibility and trust creates perfect conditions for enduring learning. When there is a need to avoid repeating errors, to find new ways of doing things and to create independence of thought there is a consequent need for learning and therefore coaching.

When motivation appears to be waning, it's time to coach. This can be a sure sign that the tell approach has done its job. Unless the coachee feels completely lost – in which case they'll still need a lot of direction – motivation will be higher when we involve people in what they do through coaching, fostering a sense of performance, learning and enjoyment. Look out for people beginning to question your instructions and disagreeing with your suggestions. This does not make them right and you wrong, it's just an indicator that they're beginning to think independently. Why not harness this rather than resisting it?

When the *quality* of output has become crucial, it's time to coach. There's an old saying in sports coaching along the lines of, 'you can make me run, but only I can choose to run fast'. There is a natural version of this in coaching at work along the lines of, 'you can make me work, but only I can choose to work well'. Quality of output has taken on great importance in recent years. Driven by innovations in manufacturing such as 'just in time' and 'lean production', all sorts of organisations are seeking ways to increase the quality of what they offer in line with their customer's increasing expectations. Getting a workforce to embrace quality is difficult at the best of times and downright impossible if we command them to improve quality; it doesn't work like that. In the end, the importance of quality resides in the hearts and minds of employees and thus they need convincing and to feel involved, which once again requires us to move from telling to coaching.

There are certain critical tasks, where failure would lead to disaster, that managers need to control in every detail, but these are fewer than we care to admit and for the most part coaching will get us further than telling when dealing with a team of people who have the basic skills and knowledge.

Is it a question of willingness or ability?

How would you approach coaching these characters?

John is something of an excited puppy. He works with great enthusiasm but often gives clients wrong information because he does not understand how fees are worked out. Several clients have registered complaints which makes John quite upset and you worry that his motivation and enthusiasm may wane.

Richard is a management graduate with a wide knowledge of business processes. However he is reluctant to delegate tasks and when he does he worries over his staff while they do it for him.

Georgina consistently uses inappropriate humour with customers, often coming across as sarcastic and disrespectful. She was scheduled to attend a customer care seminar but did not show up on the day.

Paul is suddenly and surprisingly becoming cynical and negative. He was once the first to embrace any new initiative, and still does, though not with the same enthusiasm. He has completed the required company training and recently passed a college diploma course, however he has just told you that he does not feel his actions have any effect on how the department operates.

- John is *willing but not able*. He has the motivation but not the skills. Use coaching to harness his motivation and create an environment where he is more willing to ask questions and seek explanations. You may need to be tolerant of his early mistakes.
- Richard is *not willing but able*. It is not that he doesn't know how to delegate; it's that he doesn't put it into practice. He does not need more training (which may just frustrate him); he needs coaching through his interferences and to find his performance, learning and enjoyment through delegation.

- Georgina is *neither willing nor able*. If you consider it is worth investing more time in her, I would suggest you start on 'willingness'. You can use coaching to try to restore motivation, but will also need to monitor her performance quite closely and provide detailed feedback. After that, it's up to her.
- Paul is *willing and able*, but may not remain so unless we provide opportunities for him to take responsibility, to do so with our trust and encourage his awareness by seeking feedback and asking for this thoughts and suggestions.

The four combinations can be arranged on a graph as in Figure 7.2.

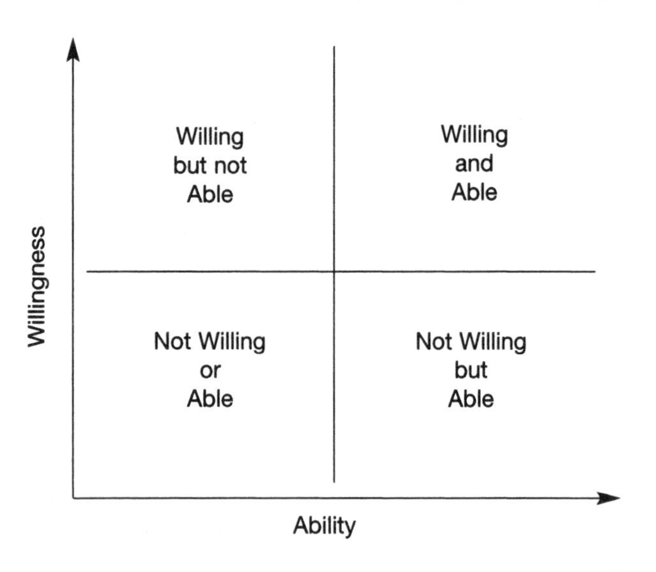

Figure 7.2: Willingness and ability

Problems of *ability* are best solved with a dose of good old-fashioned training and development. Problems with *willingness* are best dealt with through coaching. For far too long we have tried to solve problems of willingness as if they were problems of ability but this approach tends to make matters worse. Sending a highly capable but miserable salesperson on some more sales training for example, will not solve the problem.

Navigating the competency cycle

There is a well-known model that suggests that learning – or becoming competent – is a question of passing through four distinct phases. Let's attempt to see how this applies in a typical work situation.

Meet Ed. Ed is a young man who works in a conference centre. Until very recently Ed's job has been largely manual: putting the chairs in place, rearranging tables, setting up the IT equipment and sorting out flipcharts. One Friday afternoon, Ed's boss informs him that from the following Monday morning she would also like Ed to run through the domestic arrangements with groups of delegates once they have been escorted from the coffee area to the conference room.

Unconscious incompetence

That Friday evening Ed becomes a bit worried; he starts to fret about Monday. He has listened to his colleagues make the announcements hundreds of times, but he has never addressed a group before. He thinks it might be very difficult, but doesn't really know why he thinks that.

Conscious incompetence

On Monday morning, Ed takes a deep breath and begins his address. Unfortunately he forgets to mention the fire alarm test and tells the group that they will have lunch in the restaurant when in fact they are going to have a buffet in the conference room. He is so nervous that his mouth becomes dry and this makes him even more uncertain in his speech. However, he notices many of the people in the room smiling warmly at him and some even chuckle when he makes a couple of witty remarks.

Conscious competence

Over the next couple of week's it gets easier, Ed has written the points he must cover on a prompt card and finds the whole notion of addressing a group less threatening. He takes a few deep breaths and has a quiet 'chat with himself' before entering the room and this all seems to help.

Unconscious competence

Some weeks later Ed barely thinks about announcing the domestic arrangements. He has other things to worry about and when the time comes, he pops into the conference room reels off the announcements and quickly moves on to other things. To the outsider Ed looks the picture of confidence, but he does have a tendency to forget bits of information and can look a bit distracted at times.

We can similarly apply this cycle to most tasks and activities at work. The main lesson for coaching managers is to recognise that learning can only take place in the conscious – or, dare I say, aware – phases of the cycle. Thus coaching questions move people from *unconscious incompetence* to *conscious competence* but also from *unconscious competence* back to *conscious competence* to address any bad habits.

We normally let the cycle run its course, but coaching can dramatically accelerate the speed of our journey around it. We often think that we only go round the cycle once, but what would happen if we chose to repeat the cycle time and time again?

A conversation to address workplace challenges

For sake of ease, we'll return to the example of Ed and imagine that his boss, Sue, knew a thing or two about coaching and decided to have a chat with Ed about undertaking the domestic announcements.

Sue: So I'm going to ask what might seem like a strange question, 'How will you know if you've been successful?'
Ed: Err, that is a strange question. I guess if the group looks happy and if I feel happy too.
Sue: Happy's a bit woolly Ed, what exactly will you look for?
Ed: Well, I'd expect to see the group smiling and looking relaxed and I won't feel nervous.
Sue: How will you feel then?
Ed: I suppose confident and relaxed.

Sue's questions have helped Ed define an Aim in terms of what success will feel like. Her questions are raising Ed's awareness of those feelings such that he's likely to focus on them rather than his nervousness.

Sue: How do you feel about it at the moment though, Ed?
Ed: Well, I'm a bit uptight to be honest. I'm not used to this and I know Brian does it like falling off a log, but I'm not used to speaking to groups.
Sue: Have you ever done anything similar?

Ed: Actually, when I was at school I often used to have to take parents around on open evenings. We'd go from class to class and I'd have to explain the different things that went on.

Sue: What did you notice when you did that?

Ed: What did I notice? That's another strange question. I was confident enough I suppose, it's just that I couldn't remember what I had to say.

In exploring the reality Sue has encouraged Ed to become better *aware* of what exactly he experiences in these situations.

Sue: So, how big is the difference between what you felt then and how you want to feel on Monday?

Ed: You know, it's not that big actually, it's just remembering what to say.

Sue's Reflection questions are quite subtle, but the reflecting is happening nonetheless.

Sue: What could you do about that then, Ed?

Ed: Well, it's just spending time memorising the routine I suppose. I'll do some homework over the weekend.

Sue: What else could you try?

Ed: I don't know. Nothing I can think of.

Sue: What if you had to give the announcement right now?

Ed: I'd have to write it down, perhaps on some note cards. That's a good idea anyway actually.

With just a little work Sue has encouraged Ed to think beyond the obvious option.

Sue:	So?
Ed:	Yeah, you're right Sue. If I jot a few prompts on an index card I'll not worry about forgetting things and that'll make me feel a lot better. Thanks for the suggestion.

Sue decides not to tell Ed that actually this was a Way Forward he decided for himself; that he is *responsible*. She feels encouraged enough that she has his *trust*.

We can also see that although Sue is clearly using the ARROW structure, she is using questions in her own style and in a much more conversational way.

A conversation to restore motivation

Remember Richard from earlier on? We learnt that he is reluctant to delegate and worries over his staff while they do tasks for him. We decided that Richard fitted the *not willing but able* description because he understands *how* to delegate, but doesn't put it into practice. How can we motivate him to take up delegation? Pay him more? Threaten him with dire consequences? It seems unlikely that these approaches would do much good in the long term, so let's see what a coaching conversation might produce. We'll assume that the subject of Richard needing to delegate more has arisen at his staff appraisal with his manager, Brian.

Brian:	Looking at last year's notes, I see that my predecessor discussed the idea of you delegating more work. How's that been going?
Richard:	All right I suppose, but I don't like doing it if I'm honest. I worry that things will go wrong.
Brian:	How often does that happen?
Richard:	What, how often do things actually go wrong?
Brian:	Well, we might come on to that, but actually I was wondering how often you *worry* about delegating?
Richard:	Oh right. Err, not all the time, you know? It's just when it's really important stuff and where we'll be in trouble if mistakes are made?
Brian:	How does that make you feel?
Richard:	Well, it's not good is it? I mean anyone can delegate if the result doesn't matter.

Notice how Brian has started at the Reality stage because he wants to understand what has happened with Richard's efforts so far. His coaching questions are increasing Richard's awareness of his feelings regarding delegation and are uncovering his dilemma of knowing what he *should* do but worrying about the results.

Brian:	What would it be like if you didn't have these problems?
Richard:	It would be great, I could get the team doing more of the important stuff and get on with my development projects.
Brian:	How would you need to be?
Richard:	I don't get you?
Brian:	How would your behaviour need to change?

Richard: Oh right. I'd need to be more confident in setting out the requirements to the team and I suppose I'd need to be, more confident in myself to just let it be once I've delegated.

Brian: OK, when would you like to have become this 'confident delegator'?

Richard: Hmmm. Let's say in three months.

Brian may feel like going into more detail, but has succeeded already in helping Richard become aware of a worthwhile Aim. We'll assume that on Reflection Brian and Richard agree that this is a realistic Aim and join them at the Options stage.

Brian: What could you do then Richard?

Richard: Well, last year they arranged a delegation seminar, but that didn't really help. I'd covered all the theory before.

Brian: So, what else could you try?

Richard: Well, this conversation's helped me realise that the problem is really in my own head; it's because I worry about the consequences. I reckon I could delegate some of the worry too. I need to make sure that whoever I delegate tasks to is aware of the consequences and that they need to help me come up with a contingency plan in case things do go wrong.

As Richard has become more Aware of the true nature of his issue, his motivation has increased alongside the realisation that he can take steps to change his situation. Notice that it has only taken

Brian two questions at the Options stage to generate a flow of fresh ideas. They simply need to agree a few action steps and timings at the Way Forward stage and Brian can allow Richard to go and implement his plan.

A conversation to help cope with change

I'd like you to meet Nat. Nat runs the Accounts Department in a small engineering company. Until quite recently he reported to the founder and owner of the business, Valerie. They had a great relationship with few formal controls and Nat was free to do more or less as he pleased as long as the job got done. Around six months ago, Valerie sold the business to a larger engineering firm and Nat now reports to the new Managing Director, Glen.

Glen has become concerned about Nat. He sees him questioning the change all the time and longing for the 'good old days'. Nat seems to have lost his focus and his staff claim he is becoming erratic.

Glen has invited Nat to join him for lunch in a quiet corner of the work's canteen.

Glen: How's it going then?

Nat: All right.

Glen: Look Nat, I know the recent changes have made you uncomfortable. The last time we spoke you said that you thought we were just becoming 'busy fools'. You resisting things in this way makes me feel as if I'm not going to have your support and I need your support if we're going to hit the revised targets.

Glen has recognised that before the real coaching work can begin there needs to be acknowledgement of an underlying problem. Some may have been tempted to start lecturing Nat on the wider issues, the drivers for the change and the improvements planned, but Glen realises that he must demonstrate a willingness to listen to why Nat is showing resistance to change.

Nat:	You do have my support, it's just that things are so different now. I'm always being asked to report back and I seem to spend every waking hour filling in new forms.
Glen:	Always?
Nat:	Well no of course not literally all the time, but there's just so much more red tape now. It never used to be like this.
Glen:	How do your team feel?
Nat	I'm not sure really, they don't say a lot. I'm sure they feel the same way.
Glen:	What do you think needs to happen?
Nat:	I think it's all been a bit much too soon. Perhaps if we could just introduce things a bit more slowly.

Glen is encouraging Nat to explore the Reality (and in a real life situation he'd want to go into more depth) and he is now gently encouraging Nat to set his sights on a more positive Aim.

Glen: Are you being completely honest with me here, Nat?

Nat: Yes. Absolutely.

Glen: OK. You realise that I have to follow new procedures too, but I do understand your concerns. What do you think we could specifically do?

Nat: Well, take the monthly purchase ledger stats for a start. Those figures are on the system anyway so it's duplicating work... Could we not just stop that one?

Glen: Wendy asked for that but she may not have realised the figures were already available. Do me a favour and ring her directly on that one would you?

Nat: Sure, no problem.

Glen: What else could you try, Nat?

Nat: When you asked about the team I realised I hadn't really taken time to get their views. I'll talk to them too.

Glen: That sounds like a good idea. Let's talk again when you've had time to do that.

This conversation has not followed the coaching ARROW slavishly in any way, but all the steps are there. Glen has effectively used coaching to encourage Nat to raise his *awareness* of the things that are interfering with his accepting the recent changes. They'll undoubtedly need further conversations, but they've made a solid start.

A conversation to build on strengths

Ed had problems coping with nerves, Richard had problems with delegation and Nat had problems adapting to change. I've fallen for the same trap I warned you of earlier. I am focusing too much on coaching as a means of restoring performance not developing performance or building on strengths. Let's look at that now.

Curtis runs a small consultancy business providing a range of support and training for owners and managers of small to medium enterprises (SMEs). Last year he employed Elaine as a personal assistant. Elaine has a wealth of experience and had a good career with one of the large oil companies before leaving to have a family. Recently Elaine has been taking a real interest in helping Curtis build the business and has been accompanying him to client meetings. She has also been researching – on her own initiative – ways they could use technology and the Internet in the business. They are having their customary morning coffee.

Elaine:	I notice that you're due to see Johnston technologies this afternoon.
Curtis:	Yes, that's right. I could do without it to be honest, we've that much on already.
Elaine:	I could go.
Curtis:	OK, let's talk that through. What do you think you should aim to get from the meeting?
Elaine:	To get him to sign up for the three month support package!
Curtis:	Well that would be nice as a sort of maximum, but what would be the minimum you'd want to achieve?
Elaine:	Err. I suppose if I left just having made a good impression and with his agreement to continue meeting with us that would be something.
Curtis:	Yes. It would. Expecting to get a sale every meeting perhaps creates too much pressure.

So, here we have the makings of a good set of Aims.

Curtis:	What have you noticed about the meetings you've attended with me?
Elaine:	Well, don't take this the wrong way, but I think you can be a bit too soft sometimes. I'm not sure you always spot that they're ready to buy.
Curtis:	Really? What do you notice that I don't?
Elaine:	It's often in the body language. I see them leaning forward and maintaining eye contact for longer. It also seems to me that their questions are about what happens when the package of support is drawing to a close. That has to be a buying signal.
Curtis:	You're right Elaine, and I think you might have a real talent for this.

Reality has been explored and it's clear that the Aim remains viable without the need for deep reflection.

Curtis:	So, how will you play it this afternoon Elaine?
Elaine:	Well, I could take our brochure, but I'm not sure he's ready for all that detail. I was thinking that I'd have it with me but just get him talking about his business at first and look for signs that we can help. I also wondered about seeing if he'd like to help us trial the member's area of the website.

We can leave them to it now and Elaine is clearly thinking well and generating her own options without too much prompting from Curtis. All that remains is to decide which options to choose as the way forward and for Elaine to give it her best shot at the client meeting.

Someone in Elaine's position is a joy to coach as they are showing so much responsibility and initiative anyway, but we still need to make sure that everything has been thought through.

Curtis has shown good coaching skills in that he has not over-coached by asking Elaine too many questions, and he has not let his ego get in the way when she was explaining that she noticed him missing sales opportunities. As a businessman Curtis realises that Elaine has skills and assets that he can really benefit from if he cultivates them in the right way.

A conversation that uses 'tell' in a coaching style

Finally, a quick, task-focused exchange. Here's the gist of a conversation I once had with a member of my team, Angie.

Matt: Angie, I need you to finish preparing that slide presentation by 5 p.m., so I can send it to the client before he goes home.

Angie: OK, I'll get on to it straight away.

Matt: Great. When you're doing it, see if you can work out how to include a video clip. We don't actually need it for this one, but it would be nice. Do you think there's time?

Angie: Well, I'll finish what we definitely need for the client first and then look at the video thing if there's time.

Matt: Great. It'll be so useful for other presentations if we can take the time to learn about it now. Tell you what, you get on with that and I'll make the coffees this afternoon.

Here we can see that in addition to passing on an instruction and inviting my team member to perform I am also looking to see if I can let the opportunity double up into a learning and enjoyment experience too. This won't always be possible of course, some deadlines are just too fearsome, but it's surprising just how many opportunities there are to coach, once we raise our awareness of them.

Summary

This chapter has set about establishing that the time for coaching is now. Most situations at work are a coaching opportunity, either at the time or when a crisis has passed. We just need to look. At the risk of repeating myself, I want to stress again that it is not only problem situations at work that provide coaching opportunities. What would happen if we started playing to strengths? Is it best for the team and the business for everyone to be an identikit employee with the same skill profile, or should we use coaching to create unique profiles?

There's been much talk in HR circles in recent years about the need for businesses to become learning organisations. There are many facets to learning organisations, but management style is undoubtedly a foundation stone. We can use coaching to establish that learning can happen alongside the need to perform and achieve results. We can use coaching to illustrate that learning and performing are not mutually exclusive.

It has been said that high performers are simply those individuals that learn faster. If this is true it further strengthens the need for the coaching approach as we can readily see the business benefits that accrue for accelerating the process of learning from our work.

Coaching is about having the experience and learning from the experience. When we can make the experience enjoyable too we have a potent cocktail for sustainable high performance. Coaching is about moving forward; taking the next step. It is useful in virtually all aspects of working life. Its limitations are only those in the mind of the coaching manager. What internal interference do you experience when you consider the uses of coaching in your organisation?

INSTANT TIP

When somebody new joins your team, decide in advance when you would like to move from telling to coaching. Put a date in the diary. This doesn't mean that the date can't change but it will continually raise your awareness of how your newcomer is developing.

08

How do I structure and run a session?

Introduction

In this chapter I want to concentrate on the practicalities of scheduling and running coaching sessions or conducting coaching conversations. We need to consider what needs to happen before, during and after coaching to give us the best chance of achieving a successful outcome. These considerations range from the seemingly simple (though often frustratingly difficult) matter of booking an appropriate meeting room, to more complex and subtle concerns, like handling emotion.

Before we do that though, I want to examine in a little more detail what precisely is meant by a coaching session. The term covers many different ways of providing a basis for coaching and we may sometimes need to decide which way is best. So let's look at the options:

- **Scheduled v. spontaneous.** Is it best to have a coaching session pre-arranged and entered in the diaries or should we just invoke a coaching approach when the need arises? You'll not be surprised when I say that there is no right answer, it depends on the needs of the situation and the people concerned. In a busy working environment, scheduled sessions can be a good way to ensure time is 'ring fenced' to talk about long-term developmental matters, time that would otherwise be taken up by day-to-day issues. On the other hand, scheduled sessions can seem a bit heavy-handed and our people might prefer to capture a moment and have a coaching conversation just before or just after a key incident.
- **Formal v. informal.** Similarly, do we sit people down and announce that coaching has commenced or do we just get on with it knowing that our intentions are sound? Much will depend on the relationship you have with your team. If you want to signal a deliberate change of pace or management style you may want to err on the side of more formal sessions. Where you have more established, trusting relationships you can pretty much slip into the coaching approach at will.
- **Separate v. part of something else.** Should coaching be a stand alone activity or woven into some other business process such as appraisal? Once again, there is no hard and fast rule, but, unless coaching is a natural part of the other discussion and you're going to be talking about learning and improvement, I think you're better off doing it separately. It would be difficult for example to include coaching as part of a disciplinary meeting. The coaching would be better afterwards when the person concerned has had time to take in what they're being told and choose (perhaps) to do something about it.

- **Requested v. arranged.** In the ideal world coaching would only happen when people requested it because this is most in keeping with the principle of responsibility. However, most coaching in a work context needs to be arranged by the coach or the manager until it has taken root as a legitimate part of day-to-day business.
- **In depth v. quick and dirty.** Deciding whether to go into great detail or just have a quick conversation is a matter of time and appropriateness. Awareness, responsibility and trust can take time to establish, so where we can go in deep we should. On the other hand, let's not dismiss how useful a quick conversation and a few judicious coaching questions can be.

Define roles and responsibilities

This may seem at first glance to be something of a nonsense heading. Roles and responsibilities in coaching are obvious and implied in everything we've examined so far: we coach, they learn. Simple.

But is anything ever quite so straightforward in organisational life?

Coaching never happens in a vacuum. If you're coaching your own team member it may seem that only the two of you are involved, but that's probably a mistaken assumption. I'm guessing your boss will be very interested in the outcome of any coaching sessions as they too will undoubtedly benefit from improved results and they'll also be keen to see how you're developing. What about the colleagues of the team members you coach? It may be that they have a stake in the outcome too or you may have to seek their support to accommodate the learning needs of your current coachee.

If you're coaching people from outside your reporting line (and this is well worth considering) you can bet that those coachees' direct line managers will want to be involved. Deciding how much detail you can tell them about things discussed in coaching their staff is quite delicate. On the one hand you'll want to treat things discussed in coaching as confidential, but on the other hand they do have a right to know what's going on in their teams.

It seems our key principle of trust offers the best solution and suggests that the stakeholders in any coaching relationship should get together and establish some ground rules. To take a typical example, this may mean you, your coachee and their boss – if that's not you – agreeing matters like: how often coaching will take place, what will be reported, how action points that emerge from coaching sessions will be accommodated in the work schedule and so on. This seems to be the best way to make sure that all parties are agreed on how the relationship will work and avoids any conflict down the line. Attendance at such meetings may need to be extended sometimes to include members of the HR or Learning and Development departments who may have been given responsibility for establishing a coaching culture and need to monitor how that's progressing.

I think it's worth stressing that coachees have a high degree of responsibility for making coaching successful and that this needs to be emphasised from the start. Coachees need to engage in the coaching conversations with enthusiasm, give well thought-out answers to coaching questions, be prepared to challenge their limiting beliefs and be willing to try some ways forward that might make for a little discomfort. If we do not stress the active role that coachees have to play we run the risk of making ourselves, as coaches, responsible for the outcome. This is unfair. You can lead a horse to water but you cannot make it drink, so the saying goes. In the same way you can provide a climate and a structure for coaching but in the end it is the coachees that will need to make changes.

Get the setting right

On a more practical level, we need also to think about the physical location for a coaching session.

On our coaching skills programmes we encourage our participants to do their coaching practice outside wherever possible and weather permitting. This is not just to give people a good time (although coaching is undoubtedly more successful when it's enjoyable) but to recognise that successful coaching requires people to feel at ease and free from distractions. Remember that one of our main intentions is to use coaching to promote high-quality thinking, so we need an environment that can help.

When you become skilled at coaching you'll be able to coach pretty much anywhere and anytime, but to begin with it's probably best to hold coaching sessions in a separate room or office.

The primary consideration needs to be how easy it is for each of you to listen in the room you've chosen. And remember that in coaching we are seeking to employ a level of listening that requires much more focus and concentration than when we are in normal conversation. Try to avoid large glass windows in open plan meeting rooms that look out into other people's work areas or that have lots of people walking by. This just creates too many distractions. You'll also want somewhere that is completely private. Nobody is going to give really meaningful, honest answers to coaching questions if they fear that they're going to be overheard.

Other practical matters include finding some seating that is comfortable and appropriate. The typical chairs used in training rooms are maybe a bit too stiff, but big fluffy armchairs that you sink into until your knees are level with your chin are no use either! I also like a room that has natural daylight and where you can open a window for some fresh air if needs be. If not, air conditioning is probably essential.

I always find it useful to have some 'thinking tools' with me. I'll always have a stock of pens and paper for us each to write on, but

I also like to have a flipchart so that I can write or draw some large impactful images that my coachee and I can both look at and add to in an interactive way.

I am mindful of how challenging it can be to find meeting rooms in organisations these days and that what I've written provides an idealised description. People often ask me if it's all right to coach off-site and I feel it is, if both coach and coachee and truly comfortable. You need to get as close to the criteria I've outlined as possible and accept that the coaching will be a little trickier where you can't. In the end it's about finding a setting that will be a positive anchor. By this I mean that the places in which coaching takes place should be associated with high performance. Over time it is quite possible for people to feel more motivated and resourceful just by being in these places.

Hold an initial meeting

Having defined roles and responsibilities and found an appropriate setting, it's time to get together with your coachee for an introductory meeting. If you're coaching the same people whom you manage, this meeting will be about introducing the concept of coaching, explaining why you're using it now and setting out what you hope it will achieve. If you're coaching people with whom you don't normally work, this meeting is about establishing a working relationship. Let's consider both these scenarios in turn as there are common elements to both.

Here we meet Simon, Head of Sales for an office supplies company. He has decided to implement some coaching skills training he has received and is talking now to Catriona, a member of the sales team.

Simon:	So Cat, what I want us to do is to make coaching a feature of our regular get-togethers. I've had some training in this recently and would like to start coaching you and other members of the team so that we can hit this year's tough targets.
Catriona:	Fancy a tracksuit and a stopwatch do you?
Simon:	Well, I suppose I am on the field of play with you so to speak, so it is similar.
Catriona:	Actually, I was reading about a life coach in my Mum's magazine. Are you going to help us lose weight or stop smoking?
Simon:	Is that what you want?
Catriona:	Look, I'm sorry to mess about, but it's just another buzz word isn't it? It's a long time since you were on the road Simon and things have changed. I'm not sure what you can tell us.
Simon:	I don't intend telling you anything. I want to make sure you all get the most from every customer experience. I think if we're going to have any chance with these targets we're all going to need to be learning more quickly. Coaching will help us do that.
Catriona:	OK, tell me a bit more.

Now here's Karen, a Finance Manager who is meeting with Alex from IT.

Karen:	Hi Alex. I just thought we should get together and see how we get along before we think of anything more formal. How's that sound?
Alex:	Sure.
Karen:	I've made a list of the things I think we need to cover: how often we should meet, how long we should block out for the sessions, what we should do after the first three months and what records, if any, we should keep. Is there anything else?
Alex:	Err, not really.
Karen:	Are you sure? If this is going to work it has to be a joint commitment, Alex.
Alex:	Actually, I was wondering whether we could do some of this by phone or even by e-mail.
Karen:	Phone would be OK, but e-mail wouldn't really be interactive enough. Besides, I'm having real problems with my PC just now, the screen keeps freezing.
Alex:	Oh right. Have you tried switching it off and on again?

These conversations are both just snippets of what could be covered, but they give a flavour of an initial meeting in a coaching style.

Devote time to goal setting

There is a famous story…

In 1953, researchers surveyed Yale's graduating seniors to determine how many of them had specific, written goals for their future. The answer: 3 per cent. Twenty years later, researchers polled the surviving members of the Class of 1953 – and found that the 3 per cent with 'written goals' had accumulated more personal financial wealth than the other 97 per cent of the class combined!

I don't imagine there's a book on coaching that doesn't emphasise the importance of goal setting. Indeed we've already considered it here and examined the place of goals within an overall set of aims. The first part of the ARROW sequence is devoted to considering Aims, with the setting of well-formed goals an essential part of deciding how we specify success.

The Yale story goes some way to explaining the fixation with goal setting because it seems to prove the link with success, but why should this be so? Many believe it's to do with activating something like a universal consciousness, that if you focus enough on what you want it will magically appear. Some self-help books even suggest that if your desire for a parking space is strong enough you will always find one free, but it doesn't work for me. My experience suggests the explanation is much more mundane.

It is our key principle of awareness at work once more. The more aware I am of my goal the more I notice factors in my situation that will lead me towards it; my brain automatically filters out stimulus not in keeping with my goal. If I set you a goal of spotting six yellow cars on your journey home, you may not notice that number, but you'll see more than you would otherwise! We may not achieve our goals in full, but we'll achieve more than we would without them.

By the way, despite it being a staple for motivational speakers for years, it appears the Yale story may be bogus. Nobody can find the original study. More evidence for the power of beliefs perhaps?

Handle emotion

You can never legislate for what might happen once we sit people down and start asking coaching questions. It's quite possible that difficulties outside work may surface and that things get a little emotional. This is perfectly normal and can be taken as a sign that your coaching – and your own coaching style – is proving effective. It's unlikely that your coachees would disclose unsettling information if they didn't trust in your ability to help them handle it.

It's important though to make sure that you're both comfortable in moving forward if coaching goes from simple task-related issues, into emotional territory such as anger, fear, sadness, shame or jealousy. If you are very uncomfortable in dealing with such topics you'd be best advised to end the coaching session gently by explaining that you feel things have moved outside the boundaries of coaching and work with your coachee in finding other forms of support. If you feel comfortable then you can continue coaching, but it's wise to seek the coachee's 'permission' by saying something along the lines of, 'We appear to be getting into emotional elements here, are you happy to continue?' If you have experience of the same emotions it can be useful to disclose this to the coachee and it often strengthens trust. Remember though that their own experience is unique.

You can raise awareness by challenging what you think might be 'false' emotions. A senior manager may be very 'hurt' but describe her feelings as 'angry' as this sounds less vulnerable. It is also useful to reflect the emotions you observe. This may mean saying, 'I notice that when we talk about the merger, your posture changes and your voice quietens. I'm guessing you're very upset by all this'. Doing this signals that an emotional reaction is perfectly normal and allows the coachee to challenge your assumptions: 'No, I'm not upset at all; it's just that...'. This raises their awareness and deepens their focus.

Consider role-playing

A point of clarification. I do not mean the use of traditional role-playing as experienced (usually painfully) by delegates on sales training courses or similar. I am not about to suggest that you and your coachee develop a script and set up video cameras. By role-playing I mean the idea of experimenting and trying ideas 'on for size'. There are two main ways in which this is helpful in a coaching session.

Firstly we can offer our coachees the idea of 'practice without penalty'. If, for example, they have come up with a Way Forward that involves asserting their rights in response to an aggressive colleague, then you can adopt the role of the colleague and they can try out what they want to say to see what happens. Of course it won't be real, that's not the point. It's simply a chance to move gently out of a comfort zone before the real thing. It can also be quite therapeutic to say exactly what they want to say with no fear of the consequences!

The other good use of role-playing is where you become the coachee and they put themselves in the position of the other person with whom they are having difficulty. A great awareness raising tool and a really effective way of challenging perceptions and building empathy.

Identify unhelpful habits

Prominent amongst any list of internal interference will be the notion of unhelpful habits. We all of us have habits of thought and behaviour – they can be thought of as our tendency to respond to things in a certain way. When we describe other people as domineering or shy we are simply indicating that this is the way in which that person habitually responds. Much of this is subtle stuff indeed and it would be true to say that there are more habits than those that have names. In fact, naming habits can sometimes be unhelpful as names come with value judgements around things being 'good' or 'bad'. In coaching it's far more useful to consider actual behaviour and examine the extent to which it is helpful or unhelpful.

We all have an endless number of habits, but we may not be consciously aware of them. As a coach you might notice that someone is habitually late for meetings, but they might not see that as a habit and be able to produce a whole list of reasons why they couldn't help being late 'this one time'. I remember being told by a manager that I had a habit of procrastinating which was bad, and I remember disputing this with great vigour. However I can also remember being invited by my coach to consider the pros and cons of putting things off, which was much more helpful.

In the spirit of raising non-judgemental awareness, our job as a coach is to help people notice the effects of their behaviour rather than try to force them to change. Remember that aspects of some habits are really helpful and not something that should be lost. The person habitually late for meetings for example may have developed habits in terms of preparing very quickly and picking out key information. It can be useful to offer your observations to the coachee by saying, 'I've noticed that...'. You can them move on to Reality questions around how much or how often the behaviour occurs.

Follow-up

If you're reading this as a coaching manager rather than an independent coach, you have an advantage. It is much easier for you to follow up and keep in contact with your coachees. This has real advantages when it comes to coaching on, say, unhelpful habits because change of this type responds better to a regular series of short sessions than it does to weighty, single sessions. This is obviously easier to achieve when you're working alongside people day by day.

Let's pick up with Elaine and Curtis. You'll remember that Elaine was going to meet with Johnston Technologies and that Curtis had been coaching her so that she was fully focused. Here they are having their coffee the next morning.

Curtis:	How did you get on?
Elaine:	OK, I suppose, but he didn't sign up for the three month support package.
Curtis:	How soon did you realise that?
Elaine:	Pardon me?
Curtis:	How soon in the conversation did you realise he wasn't going to sign up?
Elaine:	I'm not sure I understand. When I asked him if he was ready to commit he said no. That was at the end of the conversation.
Curtis:	Were you surprised?
Elaine:	I wasn't actually.
Curtis:	How come?
Elaine:	Well, now you mention it I could tell by his body language after about five minutes. He'd said earlier on that he was a bit wary of training companies, but I pressed on. About five minutes in he just glazed over.
Curtis:	Did you change your approach?
Elaine:	No I didn't, because I wasn't really sure what to do.
Curtis:	So, what if that happens again?
Elaine:	Well, I hope it doesn't, but I think I'd acknowledge what was happening and ask if everything was clear or if he had any comments he wanted to raise before we went on.
Curtis:	That sounds like a good idea. Well done. How did you feel at the end of the meeting?
Elaine:	Well, he did say he would definitely be back in touch, so I must have made that good impression I wanted to!

We can see that Curtis has used coaching questions to make sure Elaine has learnt a great deal from her experience and invited her to realise that some things went very well too.

Summary

As we said in the introduction to this chapter, there is a clear beginning, middle and end to a coaching session. Before you and your coachee can sit down and have a coaching conversation in the way I've described in this book, there are certain things that you'll need to agree. It will be important to think through the degree of formality you want for coaching in your organisation and that extends to thinking in advance about how long sessions might last and how often you'll meet. It is wise to think through the roles and responsibilities of the various parties involved and to do this in advance to avoid problems later on.

Your options for coaching locations vary from a formal meeting room to the local coffee shop. Each has its advantages and disadvantages so just think about what you might need to account for and remember to make sure the coachee is comfortable with whatever you decide.

Use the coaching ARROW to provide the framework for a session and to make sure you establish useful goals and identify any unhelpful behaviour. Think about your own comfort levels in handling emotional exchanges and give thought to whether role-playing might be helpful to what you're both trying to achieve.

Make sure there is a firm Way Forward agreed before any session finishes and, where you can, take advantage of any opportunities for following up. It can be here that lasting change takes root.

INSTANT TIP

Any time you have a follow-up conversation, ask:

- What did you learn?
- How did you learn it?
- What will you do next time?

09

How can I coach my team?

Introduction

I'm guessing that if you're reading this chapter, you're part of one or more teams in your place of work. You might be in something called a Sales Team or an Admin Team. You might even be in a Senior Management Team. Your team might be temporary or permanent, based in one place or scattered across many sites. You might be the leader of one and a member of others. Work is complex and few tasks can be completed by one person working in isolation. The nature of work compels us to operate as teams to get things done.

Why then, when teams are the prevalent model for bringing people together to achieve a common goal, does it seem to be so difficult? Why do so many teams seem to fall short of what they could really achieve if they could properly harness the talents of its members? Most would argue that there has never been a greater need to deploy teams to meet business challenges, but I would contend that it seems as difficult as ever to develop a team towards high performance.

There are many reasons for this. The world of work is more complicated these days, with more complex problems requiring more complex solutions. The increasing utilisation of ephemeral project teams has seen the timescales in which teams are expected to form and perform shrink drastically. Teams these days are not always housed in the same country, let alone the same building. Furthermore 'working from home' and other flexible working patterns make it difficult for many teams to come together physically. Rigid hierarchies have collapsed and been replaced with fluid, matrix style workgroups.

My aim in this chapter is to show that coaching provides an antidote to these issues and more besides. Not because it provides some magic bullet that makes team issues disappear but because coaching, as we've seen, is concerned with enabling people to perform at their best, and teams, in the end, are nothing more than collections of people.

Furthermore, a coaching style of team leadership (or indeed team membership – the team leader need not be the only coach) is a style that is appropriate at all stages of team development, whereas other styles may prove to be ineffective as the nature of a team changes over time.

Team development

There are many frameworks of team development in popular use, with perhaps the best known being educational psychologist Bruce Tuckman's four-stage model (Forming, Storming, Norming and Performing). Personally, I prefer John Whitmore's three-stage version (Inclusion, Assertion and Cooperation – expanded on later in this chapter.)

This classic 'act in three parts' viewpoint appears throughout nature: the sun rises, hovers above us at noon then sets; as people we are born, we grow and then we die. A three-stage model then will resonate in a way which makes it very easy to relate what happens in teams with other experiences which you and your team may have worked through.

Before we consider *how* teams develop though, we'll firstly focus on the level of high performance we're aiming to move the team towards.

The qualities of a high-performing team

When discussing coaching for team development on our training courses, I will often begin by asking my participants to recall a time when they can remember feeling part of a high-performing team, and then to make a list of the qualities that team had. No two lists are ever the same, but the following qualities appear time and time again and can thus be considered core. (As an aside, it is interesting to note that during this exercise the majority of people draw on experiences outside of work. It seems that there is a long way to go before the quality of team working in organisational life matches that found in high-performing sports or other teams.)

Common goals

My experience suggests that this is the single biggest point of differentiation between a truly high-performing team and a team that is 'good enough'. We have noted the power of goals throughout this book and we know their use in providing a point of focus for the individual. Without a goal, an individual may lose their way and waste energy. Without a shared goal, members of a team work against each other as different agendas and disagreements about the way forward collide. The lack of a common goal does not merely hold the team in neutral, it creates backward momentum.

Effective leadership

The first thing to say here is that effective leadership is not the preserve of the nominated leader. In a work situation, the leader of the team is not necessarily the person with the word 'leader' in their job title. In a high-performing team, leadership has a dynamic quality; there is movement and change. A good leader will generate empowerment in the team, allowing team members to play to their strengths and exercise responsibility, but they will take control when the situation demands. A good leader will recognise that at particular times it may be another member of the group that effectively takes the lead but are not threatened by this.

Good communication

If there is any area of work that cries out for a focus on quality rather than quantity it is surely communication. 'We're hopeless at communication' staff lament on survey questionnaires or Works Council meetings. The typical management response is to issue more communication: memos, emails, staff notices and now increasingly blogs and intranet pages. We are all drowning in communication and the problem is in keeping up. In high-performing teams communication is a matter of 'less is more'. Key messages move rapidly across the team, ensuring people are clear about what they need to do and have the time and space to do it.

Diversity

A high-performing team will have a vibrant mix of skills, abilities and experiences. In a work context this extends to a vibrant mix of ages, backgrounds, nationalities, creeds and so on. I would encourage you to view this as a business imperative rather than a political nicety. A diverse team will be able to draw upon a much wider range of ideas and experiences when faced with the new and emerging challenges of our modern world. The diverse team will have the flexibility to move with the times that will leave the homogeneous team redundant.

Praise and recognition

As long as it's sincere you cannot give too much praise. Certainly a high-performing team will feature liberal doses of appreciation, constructive feedback and acknowledgement. Often this is done in a very public way whereas any problems or criticisms are aired 'in-house'.

With these qualities in mind, let's now consider how we can use coaching to develop a team towards this point.

Inclusion

Another list I often ask participants to produce, concerns their thoughts and feelings upon joining a new team for the first time. Again the following would be typical:

fearful	lost
nervous	isolated
anxious	marooned
challenged	needing assurance
excited	needing information

Notice that these feelings are introverted and largely negative. At this stage people's energy is almost entirely inwardly directed and there is little left to spare to think about team or organisational goals or matters of business strategy.

It follows that a coaching approach on its own at this stage would not work. Before they are ready to assume some personal responsibility and use their initiative, people need direction, information, guidance and reassurance. This needs to happen quickly and in most organisations is accomplished by way of an induction process. Unfortunately too many inductions consist of the new team member being whizzed round the building shaking hands and being introduced to people they will never remember and are unlikely to meet ever again. Never lose sight of the fact that a decent induction will need to take account of the *needs* and *feelings* people experience during the inclusion stage.

One of my first assignments as a consultant was to run some induction training at a large call centre. There were about ninety new recruits one Monday morning corralled in the reception area waiting to start their three-week, classroom-based induction programme. Most of these people were very young and were starting their first ever job. You could almost touch the nervousness and anxiety.

We each took thirty or so to our respective classrooms where, for the first hour, they were given a PowerPoint presentation on the call centre's mission and values. There was very little interaction and the directors giving the presentations were disappointed at the response.

The problem was this was all too much too soon. People can't concern themselves with the organisation's needs until their own, more pressing, needs have been met. In this case, this meant understanding the basics of where they would be working, what happened at lunchtime, what to do in the event of illness, etc.

Coaching at the inclusion stage is a matter of acknowledging these concerns and providing the answers. I recommend nominating an experienced team member to receive the new recruits and possibly act as their 'buddy' for the first few days. An early team meeting is also wise as it will give you the opportunity to introduce the new member to the team's ground rules and give you an opportunity to reinforce those ground rules with the existing team too.

Assertion

I think it reasonable to suggest that few teams are ever stuck at the Inclusion stage and that either by virtue of a structured induction process or by simple passage of time, Inclusion needs are met and we move on.

At the Assertion stage people's energy turns towards other team members and they begin to focus on the nature of team relationships. This will include sizing up rivals for promotion or deciding who to side with in the event of things going wrong. In larger teams of more than, say, 12 people, cliques can form. A clique is not useful for team development as it encourages a 'them and us' mentality. On the other hand, a sub-group which perhaps forms around pockets of particular expertise in a team can be useful provided it is aligned to the overall team goals.

Your management style can now afford to become less directive and you should find a wealth of ideas and contributions emerge as you adopt a more consultative approach to team communication.

If you feel your team is at this stage, I recommend that you work together on the following exercise as part of any team development activity.

Get the team together and ask everybody to list the qualities they think will be most crucial to the challenges ahead. Then get them to whittle the items down to a list of about six to ten, which you can put in priority order if you like. Ask each person to rate the team against each quality and plot the results as per the table in the case study below. The high and low scores can be quite revealing and good discussion material for resolving issues. If you like you can take this to the extreme by asking team members to rate each other individually, but this needs careful handling.

A case example

In my own firm, Peak, we regularly get together and run through the team qualities exercise. Here's one of our own charts:

	Matt	**Carol**	**Leanne**	**Lesley**	**Average**
trust	9	8	4	6	6.75
support	8	7	8	6	7.25
fun	7	5	5	7	6
integrity	9	7	8	9	7.5
focus	7	7	8	4	6.5
learning	6	6	6	7	6.25

Looking at this I can conclude that while I personally perceive high levels of trust, I need to understand why Leanne may not be having the same experience.

Similarly I should talk to Lesley to understand why she feels the team lacks focus.

Such conversations are not always comfortable, particularly if there are poor levels of trust, but we cannot move forward while such issues are unresolved and they won't go away by themselves. Hope is not a strategy!

The Assertion stage is as far as many teams ever get, but you can still get some pretty good results from people who are only competing to outdo each other inside the team. In some organisations, where internal competition is seen as a panacea for performance problems and a universal motivating force, it is almost impossible for teams to develop beyond the Assertion stage. However, such teams are usually pretty uncomfortable groups to work in and have a tendency to crack when they come under real pressure. This is because team members have not learnt to trust each other and do not know how to work with and for each other. They get 'beaten' by teams who have reached the next stage and have learnt how to produce genuine, sustainable team performance.

In coaching a team through this stage we must recognise that team members are looking for different things. Some want power and status in the team; others are looking for recognition and a sense of achievement. Coaching conversations will unveil where the balance lies. Look for ways of delegating some power and of giving some praise and recognition, and remember that this is something that all members of the team can contribute to.

Cooperation

By now you should have worked through a lot of the pain and have a group of people prepared to align to a common goal. Of course you'll need to make sure the common goal is simply and clearly articulated and communicated, and ensure – as far as is possible in a work environment – that it is in keeping with the team member's personal goals. These issues can be sorted out in individual and team coaching sessions.

By now the team will be ready and wanting to take more responsibility and you can move to a more 'pure' coaching style, asking instead of telling, giving choice and ownership and encouraging interdependent relationships. Energy will be outwardly focused which you can use to discuss and agree the team goals as outlined above.

Activities I would suggest at this point include:

- **Socialising together as a team.** This is not the universal panacea for team development some would have you believe and needs to be handled sensitively. People have commitments outside of work and wildly different ideas about what is fun and enjoyable. Nevertheless, finding something enjoyable to do together outside of work can bring benefits to the quality of working life back in the team.
- **Learn a skill together.** Now I'm biased, but I can think of no more useful skill for all team members to have than coaching. The best performing teams are surely those where everyone knows and applies a little coaching.
- **Develop and agree the team's unique ground rules.** Clive Woodward, coach of England's World Cup winning Rugby Union team creates a 'teamship' book for all the teams with whom he works. This book contains the standards, values and principles to which all team members are asked to agree. High-performing teams pay as much attention to the team process as they do to team tasks and are concerned with operating within a set of guiding principles. However, such a set of principles cannot be imposed from outside, rather they must be devised and owned by the team itself. Consequently any such document – if you take it that far – must be seen as fluid and dynamic and must be adapted to take account of new team members or changing external requirements.

No team ever reached the Cooperation stage without first experiencing Inclusion and Assertion. We can move teams quickly through those first two stages, but they cannot be bypassed or short-circuited. Glossy posters on staff room walls extolling the virtues of a cooperative approach will not work. Neither will teaching team theory or facilitating away days unless the natural, evolutionary conflicts inherent in the first two stages are dealt with.

Just because we develop a cooperative team there is no valve that prevents a team from sliding back down the development scale. A change in team membership, for example, re-introduces an element of Inclusion and Assertion that needs to be worked through.

Similarly a change in the overall goal may conflict with the personal goals of some team members which again need to be acknowledged and addressed.

You cannot just sit back and enjoy yourself once the team has reached the Cooperation stage. It requires constant maintenance and the coach's job is to facilitate this process and to monitor and maintain progress.

We can now pay attention to some of the factors that can impact the direction of team development and consider ways you can use coaching to manage the effects.

Interference

We've already examined one set of interferences, the internal and external interferences that individuals experience and which affect their ability to focus and perform at their best. In team coaching it is also useful to consider another set of interferences that often keep the team anchored at the Assertion stage, unable to move forward.

Individual interferences

Evaluation apprehension

This is essentially the fear of being evaluated and judged. Whilst most team members appreciate honest, sensitive constructive feedback, this is rarely on offer. Instead team leaders fall into the trap of labellling what people *are* rather than commenting on what they do. This causes resistance to learning and a tendency to cover mistakes.

Social loafing

This refers to the phenomenon of working less hard in a group than when working alone. For example, you don't *have* to sing at a football match – there are plenty of others that will... The main explanation for social loafing is that people feel unmotivated when working in a group, because they think that their contributions will not be noticed, but it does not occur when the group members feel that the task or the group itself is important.

To avoid it, get every member involved in the team by assigning them specific, meaningful tasks. People are very reluctant to let the team down when they have specific obligations to complete. Better yet, give the team members the opportunity to choose the task they want to fulfil. Assigning roles in a group can cause complaints and frustration. Allowing group members the freedom to choose their role makes social loafing less likely, and encourages the members to work together as a team.

Playing politics

This occurs when the team member chooses personal ambitions over team effectiveness. It is symptomatic of a team stuck at the Assertion stage with an over-emphasis on internal competition. Once again the antidote is to promote a greater focus on the common goal as it creates a move towards a bigger vision or mission.

Lip service

Nothing destroys trust – so essential to team relationships – quicker than a failure to honour agreements. To increase trust we could try *disclosing*, that is, telling others aspects about ourselves, our values and our thoughts that they do not currently know. Secondly we can be open to *feedback* so that people can raise our awareness of things we do or say without realising the effect.

Open and honest communication featuring feedback and disclosure is a quality of all effective teams and helps create a climate where lip service will never occur.

Unwillingness to communicate

As we saw when we looked at the qualities of a high-performing team, an ability to communicate effectively is a hallmark of a team that is cooperating. Conversely, an inability or indeed an unwillingness to communicate must be seen as cause for concern. It usually manifests as a lack of listening or an unwillingness to disclose. It is an area of team coaching that is best dealt with by individual, one-on-one conversation rather than group sessions.

Group interferences

Group polarisation

Do groups make better decisions than individuals? This question has plagued management researchers and team leaders alike for many years and is likely to prove just as perplexing for those of us interested in team coaching. If 'two heads are better than one' as the saying goes, it follows that many heads should reach better decisions given the different viewpoints and experiences that can be drawn upon. This would be true were it not for the phenomenon of group polarisation, which occurs when two opposite positions are put forth and team members 'polarise' or take sides.

It can result in a paralysis in decision-making and an unwillingness to participate. Eventually, it can lead to groupthink, where the main views and decisions of the group override individual views. The pressure to agree decisions and hit timescales suppresses dissent and the cool appraisal of other options, leading to conformity.

To avoid group polarisation and groupthink, leaders need to be non-directive and thus a coaching style offers the best results. All members of the team should be encouraged to contribute views and this should be contrived if necessary. As the team coach you should be prepared to play 'Devil's advocate' from time to time to ensure all views are considered.

Poor decisions

At the same time we must recognise decisions made in this consultative way may take longer to reach. We need to guard against the team agreeing to a course of action that individually none of them would have backed. This means working hard to reach a consensus rather than a compromise and avoiding the 'majority vote'.

Small thinking

This occurs when the team seeks to reach consensus based on keeping everybody happy rather than on the most productive solution. As with individual coaching, when discussing options and solutions we need to be wary of stopping at the first answer and stopping at the 'right' answer.

Often it is enough to simply raise the teams' awareness of these interferences and leave them to decide how to resolve them for themselves. On other occasions you will need to encourage the team to focus instead on the team goals in order to lessen the distracting effect of these interferences.

Communicating in teams

Right from the start of this chapter we've seen that great communication is a component of the high-performing team and that it is the quality of that communication rather than the quantity that counts.

There are countless models and theories on team communication and group behaviour to guide you, but I find the categories put forward by Neil Rackham in *Behaviour Analysis in Training* (McGraw Hill, 1976) to be most closely aligned with coaching principles.

In his original research, Rackham identified 15 separate communication behaviours that distinguished the super successful managers from the merely successful. We can extend that thought to recognise that all members of a group communicate, not just the managers, so the behaviours which follow can be utilised by everyone. Note that none of the items on the list that follows is right or wrong in and of itself; it's more a question of appropriateness and context, and which are most conducive to building a high-performing team. Experience suggests that 15 is too large a number to work with practically, so I'll show the eight main categories:

seeking information	asking questions to find out what people think
bringing in	used to involve a quiet member of the team in the conversation; normally includes using their name
testing understanding	making certain that you have *really* understood another's contribution, usually by asking questions
proposing	suggesting something on which the team can take action: 'it's really cold today' is not a proposal, but 'let's turn up the heating' is
giving information	offering views and making statements
shutting out	any way in which you stop another person from contributing; it can include interruptions, side conversations, asking a question of one person but letting another answer, etc.; it can be very subtle
disagreeing	anything that says you can't go along with what's being proposed or stated
defending/attacking	graduating from disagreeing; getting off the topic and talking about the person: 'Why can't you ever make a sensible suggestion?' is one example; it usually results in the other party fighting back and can continue in a loop for a long time

I'd like to make some sweeping generalisations now based on my own experience. I suggest though that you experiment yourself in your own teams to see how much of this holds true in your own environment.

When shown the list of categories most people in teams would say it's desirable to do more of the communication described by the first four categories. These are people-centred, coaching style communication categories and they are also socially desirable; that is, we would like people to think of us as communicating in this way. They are also the types of behaviour that Rackham noted were used often by super successful managers.

In reality, when observed, most teams operate with the reverse. In meetings in particular they do lots and lots of *proposing*, and *giving information* and relatively little *testing understanding* and *bringing in*. When things get heated or there is the pressure of a looming deadline you will also see much *disagreeing* and *defending/attacking*.

It is again symptomatic of the team caught at the Assertion stage but responds well to team coaching with an emphasis on raising group awareness. One great way to do this is to nominate a communication monitor at team sessions. Give this person a sheet with the behaviours down the side and the team names across the top. Their job is to put a mark against the appropriate behaviour each time someone speaks. Provided this is then fed back with sensitivity, the team will move quite easily to the more successful communication behaviours.

Team leadership

At the start of this chapter when we considered the qualities of a high-performing team, we saw that effective leadership need not necessarily come from the nominated team leader. But working on the assumption that you probably *are* the leader in your team let's turn our sights on how to combine coaching or team development with other elements of effective leadership.

Look for tomorrow's problems and issues today

Good leaders tend to be alert, their antennae are permanently raised and they try to spot problems and opportunities early. Try to deal with problems when they are small. If, for example, team members are falling out – and this seems to be more than just the natural jockeying for position at the Assertion stage – intervene and restore communication. It won't be easy and it won't be comfortable but you'll otherwise end up having to solve a much bigger problem.

Learn to adapt to change and turn it to your advantage

In the modern world of work, nothing stays the same. Your team will find the constant change frustrating and wearing and so will you. However, you have to be the one to focus on the glass as half full rather than half empty. You have to be the eternal optimist and to see changes as opportunities rather than threats. Remember the team will model their reaction to change on yours.

Set high standards and clear goals

Before the team can align behind common goals as we described earlier, they must have common goals to work towards. Often it will be your job to create those goals, ideally working with the team to create them, but being prepared to take the lead if there is disagreement or the process is taking too long.

Create a sense of purpose

In these modern times, people are looking for far more from their work than just a living wage. Teams need to believe that their work is meaningful and worthwhile if they are to give of their best. More difficult in a commercial setting than a charitable endeavour perhaps, but every business process has a customer at the end of the chain. A person like us who must surely benefit in some way from us doing the best job we can.

Act decisively but not impulsively

Your team will respect you more if you're prepared to take a position and stand by a decision. Sometimes your decisions will be wrong and you will have to clean up the mess. Other times you'll be the hero. As long as you act in accordance with your values and can honestly say you believed you were doing the right thing, your team will back you.

Practise what you preach

Have a clear view of exactly what you think it means to be a member of that team and then be that person before you expect it of anyone else.

Keep your composure at all times

'Composed' needs to be your default setting, unfair though that may seem. Rather than worry about times when it may be appropriate to shout and swear and lose control, just don't do it. Or at the very least, don't do it in front of the team.

Provide an atmosphere of enthusiasm

Remember that the team's level of enthusiasm can never exceed your own.

Be sensitive to the needs of all team members

Finally, despite all this talk of teams, let's remember that teams are just collections of individuals who'll have their own unique set of characteristics, beliefs and values that you're seeking to gel. together Everyone has potential, everyone has a powerful contribution to make and if you coach them properly, make it they will!

Summary

By way of summary, let's round off with a number of ideas that you can put into practice straight away:

- Devote some time to team development. In any meeting or get-together of more than about an hour try to set

aside some time or extra time to discuss team development. This does not have to mean fancy management games or self-complete questionnaires. A good, honest exchange of views will bring real progress.
- Discuss the three stages of development with your team and ask them where they think they're at. Next, ask them to list the things that could take the team forward and the things that might have it moving in reverse.

John Adair, the world's leading authority on leadership and leadership development, has suggested that the successful team balances the needs of the task, the team and the individual.

Ask your team where they think the balance lies and what needs to change. Also:

- Ask your team to list all the qualities of a high-performing team and to then produce a top six in terms of what will be required in the future.
- Ask the newest member of the team to review your induction process. They will have the most recent experience.
- Catch people out doing something well and encourage all members of the team to do likewise.
- Get some instant feedback on your leadership style by asking team members to each tell one thing they'd like you to 'Stop', 'Start' and 'Continue'.

INSTANT TIP

Break with tradition. Stop celebrating success and analysing failure. Instead take up celebrating failure – because of all you'll have learnt – and analysing success!

10

What else do I need to think about?

Introduction

I think we've covered a lot of material in a short space of time. Over the course of the last nine chapters we've looked at what coaching is (and what it isn't), making a business case for coaching and motivating people to want to get involved. We've examined the attributes that good coaching managers need, some structures you can use and the principles that support them. We've even considered the practicalities of running coaching sessions, and widening the application of coaching principles to coaching in teams.

If you feel you have all you need or if you've had enough, please feel free to stop here and start on the really meaningful activity: coaching your people. As a wise man once said, it's all very well praying for potatoes, but at some point you've got to pick up a hoe!

Having said that, coaching is a massive subject and there's a lot more to say. I want to devote this last chapter to exploring some of the wider issues so that you can answer questions that people might raise and develop your coaching expertise once you're up and running. It might be that you leave this chapter until coaching has been established as part of the way you do things in your team and it becomes time to take things further.

We need to think about what it's like to be coached and the advantages to you of receiving as well as giving coaching. You may also want to think about coaching upwards and coaching your own boss.

Once you begin coaching and your success gets noticed (it will, believe me) you may be asked to champion the cause and implement coaching in your organisation. You'll then have to think about whether you'll use coaches drawn from the management ranks or whether you'll hire professional coaches. It's unlikely that you'll be successful in implementing coaching unless we acknowledge some of the obvious barriers and look at ways around them. There will be all sorts of cultural considerations too. If you work for an international organisation there are obvious cultural differences in different territories, but even a single site operation may see cultural differences between say, finance and sales.

I also want to make sure that we think through what might happen after you've finished this book so we'll spend time looking at how you determine your success as a coach. We'll also grab a crystal ball and look ahead to see how the art of coaching is set to develop in years to come and how organisations may look to further integrate the use of coaching. The final section of the book looks at how you can continue to develop your coaching skills.

Being coached

This section is predicated on the assumption that you'll value being coached as much as you value providing coaching. I have yet to come across a coaching manager who doesn't appreciate the benefits of the learning partnerships that coaches and coachees form. You will find as many opportunities to be coached as you will to provide coaching and we need to consider what it's like to be on the receiving end. This will help you get the most from a coaching relationship from a coachee perspective and also build your appreciation of the thoughts and feelings that the prospect of being coached can provoke.

Consider these reactions to the idea of being coached:

- The last thing I need is yet another person telling me what to do.
- Coach me? They've been here half the time I have!
- I don't need a coach, I can work this out myself.
- I don't want to progress. I'm happy as I am.

- My manager coaches me whether I like it or not. I don't get a choice.
- What I am really looking for is a mentor to show me the ropes.
- That's great! A coach will be able to find some good courses for me to attend.
- The senior team get coached, so why shouldn't we?

- Well I do need some help settling into my new role.
- We've really got to raise our game if we're going to meet our target.
- My career has ground to a halt. I don't really know what to do next.
- Well if it can stop me working all the hours God sends I'm all for it!

We can usefully classify these reactions in a kind of traffic light system. The first set – the red lights – are a stop signal. Our coaching will be meaningless until we acknowledge these misconceptions and take time to clarify exactly what coaching is. The second set – the amber lights – allow you to begin to coach but we must again acknowledge that something is missing. Coaching may meet these initial expectations but we should take time to highlight the real benefits that it will bring. The third set – the green lights – are your signal to get going. They represent the perfect backdrop to establishing a coaching relationship and, I'm guessing, best sum up your own thoughts to being coached.

What then can you expect to happen as a coachee? You can expect your coach to act as a sounding board, an active listener and a co-learner. They will help you clarify your needs and bring focus to your goals. You can expect to be pushed and be given 'homework' but also to be allowed to make mistakes and learn in your own way. You need in turn to be prepared to be fully involved, to design the type of relationship you'll have and decide when the coaching can ease off or stop.

We sometimes talk in terms of a person's 'coachability'. That is their readiness, willingness and ability to be coached at this moment in time. How would you rate you own coachability right now?

Coaching your boss

I am often asked, can I coach my boss?

The simple answer is yes you can and the coaching principles are exactly the same. You do however need to be subtle, making sure you don't usurp their authority and doing everything you can to work in a relationship of trust. The relationship you have with your boss is very important on both a professional and a personal level. It can have a significant influence on your day-to-day job satisfaction as well as your long-term career success. The relationship is also important to your boss who is counting on you, and your colleagues, to satisfy customers, meet deadlines and achieve objectives. But keeping this relationship healthy and productive is not about 'managing' your boss: it's about understanding them, and yourself, and then choosing to behave in a way that gets the best results for you, your boss and your organisation.

Only by understanding your mutual needs, styles, expectations, strengths and weaknesses can you develop a relationship that works for both of you. In any relationship what you say and do influences the other person. You can't change your boss but you can control your own behaviour. It's important, therefore, to understand what you do that either helps or hinders the relationship. Here are some actions you can take to make the relationship work.

Take responsibility for your own career and personal development

Ask for feedback and coaching throughout the year – don't just wait for performance reviews. Have a view on your own performance – what are you doing well? What do you need to improve on? Always be willing to discuss these things.

Take responsibility for coaching sessions

Not all bosses are good at holding coaching conversations, so help by being as positive as you can be, even if you don't like some of the criticism you may receive. Find out what your boss's expectations are and share your own. Tell your boss what development and support you need. Don't assume they'll automatically know.

Use your boss's time well

Your boss's time is limited so make good use of it, don't waste it. Find out if your boss is a lark (good first thing in the morning) or an owl (better later in the day) and choose your moment to raise issues and suggest coaching exchanges.

Use coaching to identify your boss's preferred working style

- How do they like to receive information – face-to-face, in writing, by email?
- How much do they like to be involved in decisions?
- How organised are they – can they cope with a little chaos?
- How comfortable are they with risk-taking?
- How 'hands-on' or 'hands-off' are they – can you use your own initiative?

Recognise and appreciate your boss's strengths

Compliment your boss when they do something you like; that way they'll learn the actions and attitudes that work for you. Remember, bosses are human and make mistakes too. If your boss is reasonable when you make a mistake then you should be prepared to do the same for them.

Internal v. external coaches

Our working assumption so far has been that coaching is something that 'managers' do to 'staff'. But which managers and what if they are not willing or able to provide coaching? Are there times when it might be better to hire an external coach?

Our first decision then is whether to look for coaches internally or externally. Each has its pros and cons as we'll see and much will depend on the overall climate into which you are trying to introduce coaching. For example, uncertainty about trust and confidentiality and an unwillingness to tackle issues that may concern performance or tenure make it difficult for very senior staff to turn to colleagues for help. It can be quite lonely in senior positions and the support of an external coach, unconcerned by internal politics can be hugely valuable. There are numerous business and executive coaches offering services and you'll need to consider the type of coach you're looking for and whether you want them to have a background in your industry or whether you'd prefer them to come with total objectivity.

If you look internally you'll need to decide whether you want line managers to coach as part of their day-to-day relationship or whether you want internal coaching, but aside from the line management relationship. In other words it might be useful to have someone from HR act as organisation coach or have managers from different departments crossing over and coaching people from entirely different areas. You might decide – and it's a currently popular choice – to recruit people to the specific role of coach.

Theoretically anyone can be a coach and there's no reason why the most junior member of staff couldn't coach the most senior, although this is understandably rare. Certainly there is no reason to assume that coaching must be anchored to the typical hierarchical structure and only ever offered as part of a superior/subordinate relationship. In fact, it is highly questionable whether this approach is one likely to bring about the best results, although we do need to consider credibility and other relationship issues alongside finding people with great coaching skills.

If you look externally you'll need to find someone with good coaching experience and a track record. These being, in my view, better qualifying criteria than coaching qualifications as there are too many spurious ones out there. You'll also want someone whose personal style fits your organisation and the prevailing culture (or not if culture *change* is what you're after!). Then there are of course matters of cost, availability and so on.

Let's summarise the pros and cons:

The manager as coach

Pros	Cons
can use coaching as part of a flexible approach	may have to play different roles
close to the performance of the team	can be difficult to find time
good understanding of team strengths	may have to succumb to short-term pressures and resort to 'command and control'

The specialist coach

Pros	Cons
can remain objective	might take time to establish rapport and trust with coaches
usually will have time to coach on complex issues	needs time to understand the organisation
not involved in internal politics	will eventually leave

The barriers to coaching

I am sad to say that I had no trouble in finding numerous barriers to coaching when I did my research for this book. Here are the top ten:

1. The organisation's culture is in conflict with coaching principles.
2. There are always other priorities.
3. Managers are uncomfortable in the coaching role.
4. Management resist being coached themselves.
5. There are too few role models.
6. Increased workloads make finding time for coaching difficult.
7. Short-term focus.
8. Performance related rewards promote performance but not learning or enjoyment.
9. People selected as coaches are unsuitable.
10. Perception that coaching is used to rectify poor performance (in a punitive way).

Rather than tackle these one by one, let's take an overview of what might be needed to overcome these barriers.

Coaches need time

There is no doubt that coaching requires an investment of time, but hopefully we can now make a convincing case that the return on investment is there. If we need to build in a little slack to accommodate coaching, it's well worth the effort and expense.

Coaches need good role models

Many mangaers are expected to be good coaches simply because they are managers, but this is unfair. Few managers have had any meaningful training in coaching skills and fewer still have ever been properly coached so they may simply not understand what is expected of them.

Coaches need positive rewards

Put simply, what gets rewarded usually gets done. If we want managers to coach we must reward them for doing so with praise and recognition and even bonuses if appropriate. Similarly, behaviour which is 'anti-coaching' needs to be publicly frowned upon.

Coaches need coaching

This includes feedback and guidance from their own bosses and wherever possible feedback from the people whom they coach too. It is also useful for those who have been trained as coaches to 'buddy up' and support each other.

Coaches need to be promoted

Those who are good at coaching should be promoted where it's warranted and other candidates turned away if they have not properly developed and coached their staff.

Coaches need to be carefully selected

High-flyers do not always have an interest in developing other people and often view weakness in others as a fault rather than a development opportunity. They do not always make good coaches even when given the right training and encouragement. We need to carefully define the attributes of high-performing coaches and select coaches on that basis.

Coaches need not be managers

I have often found that sometimes it is staff found relatively low down on the structure chart that make the best coaches. There is no logical reason for coaching to be undertaken only by line managers.

Coaching needs to be integrated

For coaching really to become the norm rather than the exception, the entire organisational culture must reflect its importance and value. This means that job descriptions should be revised to include coaching, competency frameworks updated to include coaching and appraisal forms amended to review and evaluate coaching activity.

Cultural considerations

I was once running some training in Kenya for Kenyans. I became exasperated that getting the delegates to come back to the training room after coffee breaks and lunch was like an exercise in herding cats! Some would wander back into the room and then wander out again to speak to someone else, others would be on their mobiles and seemingly quite reluctant to finish those conversations. When I stopped to think about it I realised that I was experiencing a cultural difference. My Anglo Saxon culture had taught me to operate *through time*. In other words, to be always conscious of 'what has happened before' and 'what will happen next' as well as dealing with the here and now. My Kenyan participants on the other hand had a culture that operates *in time*. This means that their consciousness was purely in the here and now. They weren't being rude by not returning promptly; they were just fully focused on the current moment. To them it would have been the height of bad manners to rush a conversation with a client in order to get back to training. Now you and I could argue forever about who was right and who was wrong, that's not the point. Different cultures have different realities and we need to work with them rather than get tied up in thoughts of right/wrong, good/bad, better/worse.

Of course when we talk about culture and how if affects the coaching relationship we need to realise that it is not just a matter of considering nationality, race or religion. We need also to take into account the cultures people may have become used to in previous employment, in education or in the home. More importantly perhaps, we need to think about the prevailing culture in our own organisations if coaching has not been the norm.

There are many dimensions to culture and we need to consider, amongst others:

Status: Do people rise through the organisation on merit or is status gained through age, length of service or qualifications?

Hierarchy: Is the culture one that values flat hierarchies with everyone free to express their views, or are people used to bosses telling everybody what to do?

Consensus: What have people been used to and how much scope is there to move up and down the communication spectrum?

Individualism: Do we apply coaching at the level of the team or the individual?

Emotion: Are the people that we coach comfortable with emotional language and very open in their discussions or more reserved, wanting the coach always to take the lead?

Of course, there are no right or wrong answers to these questions. They are simply views that we need to think about in order to give coaching its most solid platform.

Finally, if you find yourself coaching people who will be experiencing cultural change, raise awareness by having them identify the similarities and differences with their current culture, and help them to take responsibility for making any necessary adaptations.

Evaluating your success

Warning! *Coaching is about people not numbers. You will never be able to prove beyond all doubt that coaching is the sole cause of any performance improvement. To try to do so will prove exhausting and you are better off spending your energy on coaching more people.*

Notwithstanding the above, you may want – or be asked – to show that your coaching has been successful. This short section will provide some basic pointers and you can then do further research if you wish.

The ultimate type of evaluation is known as 'Return on Investment'. Here we are trying to put a financial value on any benefits that coaching has brought about and compare that to the financial cost of providing the coaching. Hopefully the benefits outweigh the costs and thus a return is demonstrated. It can get extremely complicated, but the following list gives the most common items that would be considered under each heading.

Costs

- coaching skills training
- administration, travel accommodation, etc.
- opportunity*

---

*Opportunity costs are the costs of doing something else. A salesperson taking time out to coach instead of sell would be missing their normal sales opportunities and this would be the opportunity cost.

Benefits

- increases in revenue
- decreases in costs
- increases in productivity
- improvements in quality
- increased effectiveness
- changes in attitude and behaviour
- new knowledge acquired
- new skills acquired

Note that we would obviously factor in the costs of an external coach where that is the case or you could calculate a time cost for an internal manager providing coaching if you prefer.

The costs should be fairly easy to identify or calculate, but establishing the benefits is less straightforward. You have three main sources of data: the coach, the coach's manager and the coach's staff (their coachees). These can be considered the main stakeholders in the success of coaching and I would recommend that you collect information from all three.

The tools you can use for data collection include:

- **Interviews:** You can interview all three stakeholder groups to ascertain their views on the benefits that coaching has achieved. You may like to consider pre- and post-coaching interviews as these can show a more accurate movement from one state to another.
- **Self-reports:** If both coaches and coachees keep journals of their coaching experience these can add real insight to evaluating success. However, they are very subjective, which needs to be allowed for, and can take up a lot of time in completing.

- **360-degree feedback:** Many organisations have existing 360-degree (feedback from managers, subordinates, clients, etc.) frameworks and it is usually quite straightforward to include coaching amongst the attributes on which feedback is sought.
- **Observation:** Direct observation can be very valuable, but remember that people rarely behave in an entirely natural way when being observed.

Using a blend of these approaches or using different tools over time is likely to give the best results and offer the most reliable data.

Future trends in coaching

By taking the time to read this book you have demonstrated a keen interest in this thing called coaching. What you have learned will serve you well in the future. Whilst nobody can know for certain what the future holds, the changing nature of the world of work means that coaching, far from being a passing fad, will quickly become an absolute necessity in the make-up of the modern manager.

In the future, work will have no boundaries. Forget about offices, factories, sites or branches. Forget about fixed structures, fixed hours, fixed job descriptions and fixed career paths. Who will be the competition and who will be the collaborative partner? Who really will be the customer and who really the supplier? Everything is changing and the lines around the things we know are becoming blurred. Coaching is a must, the only way of helping our people achieve focus amidst such uncertainty. But coaching too must change and evolve. We must be able to coach from distance which means tele-coaching – already popular with professional coaches – will need to be embraced by the coaching manager. The fledgling use of email coaching, which, in my view doesn't seem to work, will be overtaken by the sound, vision, and text interactions offered by web-based, instant messaging style technology. In fact it's already there, just ask the nearest teenager!

We can expect to see coaching become so much more than just a tool to improve results. People's relationship with work, the part it plays in their lives, is undergoing a revolution. Where once we were prepared to put up with an unsatisfying working life as long as we could pay the bills, we no longer seem prepared to spend such a large proportion of our lives in unfulfilling situations. In the future this will be more so. People will want their work to mean something and they'll want to work for organisations that take their place in the world seriously.

The future world of work will require more leaders and fewer managers. Those charged with achieving results through others will need to inspire, motivate, trust and empower. The need to allocate resources, distribute work, preside over work patterns and solve all the problems will be subsumed by technology or rendered redundant as natural selection favours those enterprises able to move at the speed society will demand. The notion of coaching as a stand alone, separate activity will be consigned to the archives and the idea of command and control type management that we still see today will soon seem as bizarre and outmoded as whipping slaves to build pyramids.

You should welcome these changes, for you are ahead of the game. You have seen the value of coaching and decided to find out more. The future world of work is evolving in such a way that your skills will be invaluable and much in demand. You have a lot to look forward to.

Summary

Annie is at the bar of the local pub buying a round of drinks for her team at the end of a long hard week. Chris approaches and waits alongside Annie at the bar so he can help carry the order when it arrives. Annie recruited Chris to the position of Team Leader a few months ago and has noticed that he seldom misses an opportunity to question Annie and find out what's going on.

Chris:	I saw the memo about the coaching programme you want to start, Annie. I'm keen to get involved.
Annie:	That's good; how much do you know about coaching?
Chris:	A fair bit actually. At my last place they brought in a team of external coaches. One of the managers refused to get involved though, so I took his place.
Annie:	How did you find it?
Chris:	Yeah good, I really found out a lot about myself and certainly our figures were up while they were around. Pity they couldn't stay.
Annie:	Well that's why I want our team to train as coaches. I think we need those skills as part and parcel of what we do. Not just something we buy in when there's a crisis.

The drinks arrive and they each carry a tray over to their colleagues. They pass two men sitting at a nearby table and Chris notices that they seem to be taking a keen interest in his and Annie's conversation. He ignores this for now, eager instead to continue his conversation with Annie.

Chris:	That's going to be a tough thing to get Derek to sign off on Annie. How are you going to play it?
Annie:	Actually he's up for it. A lot of his pals at the golf club have been telling him about the difference coaching has made in their business and to their game for that matter. I've not really had to sell the idea to him but I have said that if it's going to work I'm going to need

his absolute support and that he has to be willing to give it time. I've also told him it's high time that we looked at making managers accountable for the way they manage and develop their staff.

Chris notices the two men smile at this, and raise their glass to Annie. He asks her who they are.

Annie:	That's Gene and Sam. I worked for both of them over the years and...
Chris:	Don't tell me, they taught you all you know?
Annie:	Well, let's just say that they helped me learn. (*She raises her own glass in return.*) I think they knew a lot about coaching before it had even been given that label. Not that it was like that to begin with though. Did I ever tell you about the time I missed the submission deadline?

Chris shakes his head and so Annie begins one of many tales she will tell on their own mutual learning journey.

INSTANT TIP

Have at least one coaching conversation every day.

Developing your skills

Further reading

All of these books are in keeping with the coaching principles I've outlined.

Downey, M. *Effective Coaching*, Texere, London, 2003

Gallwey, T. *The Inner Game of Tennis*, Jonathan Cape, London, 1975

Gallwey, T. *The Inner Game of Work*, Orion Business, London, 2000

Kline, N. *Time to Think*, Wardlock, London, 1999

Landsberg, M. *The Tao of Coaching*, Harper Collins, London, 1997

Liebling, M. and Prior, R. *Coaching Made Easy*, Kogan Page, London, 2003

Somers, M. *Coaching at Work,* John Wiley, London, 2006

Whitmore, J. *Coaching for Performance*, Nicholas Brealey, London, 2002

Resources on the web

The web is awash with coaching resources, much of them utterly useless. At the time of writing I would suggest you look at:

www.coachingnetwork.org.uk
www.associationforcoaching.com
www.cipd.co.uk

Further training

Some coaching consultancies offer half-day seminars and some university business schools offer doctoral level programmes. There is a myriad of offerings along the scale in between. 'Buyer beware' applies and my advice would be to define carefully what you are looking for from a programme in advance and to then speak to at least three potential suppliers. For those of you who think you might like to eventually pursue coaching as an occupation, I would recommend extreme caution in deciding who to train with. Be particularly wary of anyone suggesting that they will provide a pool of ready-made clients after you have trained – the coaching market just doesn't work like that. The Coaching Network and the Association for Coaching (see web resources) both maintain lists of recognised training organisations but do not pursue a particular affiliation.

Further coaching

Coaching is an area of skill development that responds excellently to being coached. Professional coaches are encouraged to become coachees and it seems sensible that coaching managers seek out coaching too. You will find that working with another coach frees you from having to think about the process of coaching and that you'll learn a lot from the different approaches to coaching that different people take. At the same time you'll be further developing your appreciation of what it's like to be coached and signaling your commitment to learn and develop as an integral part of work. In the end we must do this before we can expect our own people to do the same, otherwise coaching is seen as 'do as I say, not as I do'.

Just do it!

Every working day provides countless opportunities to coach and I'd encourage you to seize as many of them as you can. With raised awareness you can learn as much about coaching as the people you coach are learning about themselves and their situations.

Index

COACHING

Instant TIPS

What is coaching?

“Before you do anything else, get together with the people whom you'll coach and decide on a working definition for yourselves. It doesn't matter if your version doesn't quite match an official definition but it must provide a consistent approach that everyone can follow.”

Why do we need coaching?

“Because it is still quite a new discipline, it is likely that you will need senior support in your organisation before coaching can really take off. You will have to make a case for the resources you need. Spend time finding out about the current threats and opportunities your organisation faces and make sure you show how coaching will address them.”

How do I get people to want to be coached?

“If you want to see an immediate boost in levels of motivation, jump on your PC and create a quick questionnaire for each of your team members which asks:

- What aspect of your job do you most enjoy?
- What aspect of your job do you least enjoy?
- What aspect of your job would you like to stay the same?”

How do I actually coach?

“Within the questioning style, make liberal use of ‘What else’?”

What principles are involved?

“Always remember that coaching is an a.r.t (awareness, responsibility, trust). Developing these facets in the people whom you coach will always pay dividends.”

What attributes do I need?

“Make your own list of, say, the top ten coaching qualities (better still, ask your team to prepare the list). Award yourself marks out of ten for each of them. Use the coaching questions in Chapter 3 to self-coach on the ones that will make the greatest impact.”

When should I use coaching?

“When somebody new joins your team, decide in advance when you would like to move from telling to coaching. Put a date in the diary. This doesn’t mean the date can’t change but it will continually raise your awareness of how your newcomer is developing.”

How do I structure and run a training session?

“Any time you have a follow-up conversation, ask:

- What did you learn?
- How did you learn it?
- What will you do next time?”

How can I coach my team?

“Break with tradition. Stop celebrating success and analysing failure. Instead take up celebrating failure – because of all you’ll have learnt – and analysing success!”

What else do I need to think about?

“Have at least one coaching conversation every day.”

chartered management institute
inspiring leaders

HODDER EDUCATION
PART OF HACHETTE LIVRE UK